Praise for Martine Bellen's Poetry

Martine Bellen invokes a new Muse, a new daughter of Mnemosyne, in WABAC Machine. In these poems, Time itself is the traveler—visiting epic, visiting nightmare, mischief and the Land of Heart's Desire. To Bellen, Time is a creature alive for an instant, and the instant reaches very far indeed, in every direction, even so far as the laughter of the gods.
 —Donald Revell

WABAC Machine begins innocently enough with the thought that a cat has no real name and proceeds through inexorable dream/dervish/fairy tale logic to a place (the wild?) where nouns dissolve. This is a world of radical flux where self is barely even a construction. Let's call it post-human. There is nothing academic about it. Things loom up and are always something else. Here it makes perfect sense for one "me" to say, "I sell temporary kitties in the form of reconstituted sponges."
 —Rae Armantrout

Quirky, electric poems, spare and challenging.
 —Peter Matthiessen

The poems in Martine Bellen's WABAC Machine are delicately rugged all-terrain vehicles for traversing multiple worlds. The work is magically both ornate and simple, exotic yet homespun.
 —Elaine Equi

Martine Bellen's psychological and linguistic adventures in poetry are unlike anyone else's. Celebrating the instabilities of our experience, her poems maneuver kaleidoscopically between ordinary life and myth or fairy tale, vital human concerns such as identity and dreamlike atmospheres where nothing stays as it appears for long. Her "host of unlikely divinities" display a reality that is never ordinary, always evocative.
 —Charles North

Martine Bellen's fabulous new collection GHOSTS! is a mosaic fable of descent and return in which a postmodern Cinderella who "likes to fuck and fuck" seeks a door for which she is emotionally the right size. It is a book of loss, in which lovers and fathers turn to ghosts and join with the winds, and also of redemption and recovery. The imagination fiercely demands to "re-member" what has been torn to pieces. Like the poet H.D., to whom she pays tribute in the beautiful first poem, Bellen displays purity, even gnosticism, of thought. The doors of passage swing both ways, into history (outward) and myth (inward), while retaining the texture of experience. Here are "transparencies before candles in a darkened room," a negotiation of light and darkness at the very axis of consciousness. The Biblical story of Lot's wife shows how emotionally fatal it is to gaze back at one's disasters. The doors ahead are all open, if we will only take the courage to pass through them, charged not with regret but desire.
 —Paul Hoover

When one thinks of ghosts, one imagines beings that are both literally and figuratively unresolved. Like a flickering fluorescent bulb, a ghost occupies the liminal space between life and death, presumably because of an unfulfilled need for closure. Bellen, whose *Tales of Murasaki and Other Poems* won a National Poetry Series award, carries this theme forward in her current collection with a lyricism more germane to the living than to the recently departed. Her work is unfailingly musical even while sacrificing none of the concrete details of the quotidian. When she reminds the reader that "each line in a poem can't avoid acting as a series of questions," she shows a concern for the worldly that transcends the merely personal focus of more mainstream verse.
—Chris Pusateri, *Library Journal*

[Bellen's] gradual accretive methods and early invocations of Sappho and Freud should remind more than a few readers of H.D.; the foremother of lyric poetry sponsors Bellen's melancholy victory: "The daughter of God/Chariot pulled by sparrows aquiver across high, steep air/And none alive remembers you, gray among ghosts." This poet offers not smoothly finished, closed-off verbal objects but "Raw exposures, too contrasted to reckon/Like sailing through a star."
—*Publishers Weekly*

Sketched within three series of poems, a woman's story reflects and refracts through the brackets of life and death, and the "story," as I have called it, never manages to dry into any flat sort of wholeness. How to see her? It would be like defining what Ingrid Bergman was like through the six films she made with Rossellini. What happens in *GHOSTS!* is, on the other hand, strikingly similar to what happens to Ingrid in *Europa '51* and that one with George Sanders—we change, change utterly as the words mount up to our waists like dry leaves in a red country.
—Kevin Killian

Contemporary poems on the ancient past have to be ghosts. They are dragged through the inscriptions of strangers until they become something ethereal and gray. And in that spectral light, as we know, colors become brighter as if shining from rain. This is how I read these poems and find them fresh.
—Fanny Howe

Martine Bellen's *The Vulnerability of Order* brings to contemporary poetics an acute, agile intelligence revealed in a dazzling array of linguistic orders, as vulnerable as they are powerful. Her inquiry into the nature of spirit is informed by arcs of interlocking knowledge, from a variety of religious practices to biological incidents in the lives of seven heretical women. Preceded as much by Emily Dickinson's perceptual condensation as by Marianne Moore's love for the objective real, Bellen has opened new enchantments in the oldest of human places—"what dissolves are the ordinary aspects." An extraordinary achievement.
—Ann Lauterbach

Reading Martine Bellen's extended, linked poems I think of cave fish navigating by instinct, not dependent on light. I am also reminded of labyrinths, nebulae, webs, sacs—*Places People Dare Not Enter*—of amniotic margins of thought forming in fluid suspension.
—C.D. Wright

The grander increment of detail in Martine Bellen's poetry singles her out as an ebullient scrutineer.... I admire the way she posits her poems on precisely registered detail, the artillery badges of the daily world, the correct grammar of the Latin in which our forbears expressed their puzzlement, the petty ambush of proper titles thrust on the toys of joy.
    —Paul West, *First Intensity*

A multivalent, multidirectional logic dance across categories to a space where we cannot tell if a lover "is parting or a part of mist and memory, the path is endless." It takes our breath away as it leaps across continents and centuries, from pre-Columbian Mexico to Japan, from myth to biology. Out of the intervals, out of the body of words, arises a wonderfully rich music that "never stops being magic, not quite green but it created a before, a bus stop."
    —Rosmarie Waldrop

Martine Bellen is a poet of refreshing complexity. Her unpredictable disjunctions and conjunctions and her baroque mix of vivid images and meticulous abstractions make one uncertain whether these poems (in verse composed of prose segments) are precise narrations of the contingent or of dreams or of the former masquerading as the latter. They are full of surprises.
    —Jackson Mac Low

Echoey music, sweet and provocative, is the lure in Martine Bellen's language maze, where word opens onto word as though in search of a secret exit, or perhaps just deeper harmonies, deeper allure. Language's old formal pathways, the song says, are not enough to take us places people dare not enter.
    —Robert Coover

Martine Bellen's poems dissolve the world of ordinary conversation and etch out patterns that demand another kind of world, one in which Satan is satin—but still Satan. And then it comes as something of a shock to find it's in fact our ordinary world still, which she has somehow gotten from a new angle. A real achievement.
    —Keith Waldrop

This Amazing Cage of Light:
New and Selected Poems

Martine Bellen

SPUYTEN DUYVIL
New York City

ACKNOWLEDGMENTS

The author would like to thank the following publishers/editors for first publishing the following collections:

Places People Dare Not Enter © 1991 by Martine Bellen, Poets & Poets Press.
Tales of Murasaki and Other Poems © 1999 by Martine Bellen, Sun & Moon Press.
The Vulnerability of Order © 2001 by Martine Bellen, Copper Canyon Press.
GHOSTS! © 2007 by Martine Bellen, Spuyten Duyvil Press.
WABAC Machine © 2013 by Martine Bellen, Furniture Press Books.

…And would like to thank the following editors and publishers for first publishing these pieces in the following anthologies:

"Time Travel and Poetry" was originally published in *Lyric Postmodernisms: An Anthology of Contemporary Innovative Poetics*, edited by Reginald Shepherd (Counterpoint Press: 2008).

"Fringe" was originally published in *Rabbit Ears: The First Anthology of Poetry about TV*, edited by Joel Allegretti (NYQ Books: 2015).

…And would like to thank the editors of the following journals for first publishing work in the "new poems" section: *Fairy Tale Review*, *La Vague* (www.lavaguejournal.com), *La Volta* (www.thevolta.org), and special thanks to *Conjunctions* for publishing my work from the start to the newest.

The author would like to thank Elaine Equi and Magus Magnus for their helpful comments, counsel, and friendship; Tod Thilleman for his sharp mind, patience, and enthusiasm; and my husband, James, for his unceasing encouragement and kindness.

Copyright © 2015 Martine Bellen
Copyright © 2014, Carolyn Guinzio, cover photograph: *Girl in Green 2*
Joe Gaffney, author photo
ISBN 978-1-941550-32-8

Library of Congress Cataloging-in-Publication Data

Bellen, Martine.
 [Poems. Selections]
 This amazing cage of light : new and selected poems / Martine Bellen.
   pages ; cm
 ISBN 978-1-941550-32-8 (softcover)
 I. Title.
PS3552.E5336A6 2015
811'.54--dc23

2014034406

for Robert Kelly

Table of Contents

From *Places People Dare Not Enter*

Camisado	3
Deception	4
Cistern	6
The Still-Bound	8
Hole	9
Storm	11
Sky Frames	13
Absolutely	14
Coda	18

From *Tales of Murasaki and Other Poems*

Time Travel and Poetry	21
Terrifying Creatures	23
Architectures	26
What the Animals Told	33
Tales of Murasaki	42

From *The Vulnerability of Order*

Perennials	59
Cuccina	60
White Butterfly	61
Swifts and Swallows	62
All Beasts Are Driven to Pasture	63
The Vulnerability of Order	64
Nocturne	66
Magic Musée	69
Devi	72
Foundation Mandala	77
Belle Starr	80
Pocahontas	88
Calamity Jane	97

From GHOSTS!

Tribute to H.D.	115
Spiritual Mathematics	122
Crimes of Living>The Persistence of Passion>Women in the Windows	125
Approximation of Myself>Wool and Water>Myo's Secret Delivery	127
Approximation of Myself>Wool and Water>Myo's Secret Delivery	134
Living with Animals	139
Cubist Winds	142
Dearest	146

From WABAC Machine

Cat	149
Customers Who Bought "Sleeping Beauty"	150
Hard Objects Found in People	155
The Mountain	158
The Gossamer Tincture	162
Assemblage	167
The Philosophy of House-Keeping	171
The Secret Conversing of Birds	173
Snowing Oven	175
On Becoming a Poem	176
The Composer	181
Spirited Away	183
The Moving Castle	185
Oshimai [The End]	188

New Poems

Quotations	191
Pond Animals	195
Monstrosity: The Goddess Suite	198
Mappa Mundi of the Uncharted Sea	201
The Woods	204
A Thousand and One Gretels: Alone in the Wood	207
Fringe	209
Suicide by Cartoon	211
John's Koan	212
The Day Lou Reed Died	213
Bird Calls	214

From Places People Dare Not Enter

Camisado

Across the bridge a basilisk waits for breath and your past with the weight of what you live—a complete description moves inside a universe indefinite because of finite matters. And stars unbounded by direction. No one must note the secret, though it may be known there is text stored in the solar nervous system, which we will never enter. The knowledge is possible but not its possession:

A castle deep not of this time we sought for what the dead take with them with a rigor that frightens; eyelike spot on ocelot looking nothing toward. We are drawn to the lazy pagan majesty where once a mortal error breaks the crawlspace lock all falls into the cellar. What wails lie open in this game with inner moves?

Turbulence expands universe, and black groves suck the donjon dry of ineffable drift. We enter the missing sin through water though Iris, inseparable seer, cannot dissociate wind from air on any one layer. Hold on to the rim of this linear sea.

Spheres of seen perish when washed by fire; a chorus composed of our female friends seeks the things obscene. And after his face you are no longer, but make too much of leaving the cellular by star. Being detaches itself from inversion. At bottom it may collapse onto the beach at your skull, a circumstance of mortality where every wave breaks and rejoins. What you were ends frozen across the horizon.

Deception

> *What could empty the universe of its human content?*
> *Would it take place in a moment or last?*

In the beginning the sun burned through her eye and her womb was a human hum. I carried her in my pocket one hundred and fifty days while oceans completed intuition, imagination. Crayfish appeared out the pond. Her last half hour of memory frozen in the early stages of our enfoldment.

There is an altar in her back. I placed it to feel her bend a stretch of space between cranium and moon. She closes her eyes to be in her head, wraps arms around torso to be in the body. Crosses legs and hearts. Meaning shifts out of her. She reaches around her mind for a scar, treats the place that hurts. Someone switches questions inside so she sees in a different light what entered. Meantime, monsters, monsters more resemble man, guard cathedrals she prays respect in dark only she can see. It's a shape like the pain she screams from. She might tell herself she knows in her bones it will never stop, a feeling that is her in a whisper, a two-way dream characterized by out- and inside intimate.

A situation of rememory escaped as a child and entered during a week. She walked into me, courting death. His blade up against her marked in blood where she didn't exist. When it reached her limits she blinked, when it ruptured the air—no mirage but a seeing in secret the eye under siege—a memory image of her, and there's no doubt about it being an independent film of thought with sound, pain, taste in odor coordinates that fry themselves blue. I can smell the contents coming to me; sometimes I don't recognize one and am not surprised.

In a dream she watches herself. She is traveling still, not yet arrived at structures that break without notice. A trace of experience found in the brain, a disregarded cell she haunts.

It's easier for those no longer mobile to pass through the many appearances they once wore, fading into the face; light substitutes for her person. I chart her at every quarter, and if she misses, she strays in sleep. Scream stalks her house. There's a fresh one underside surface, a depth before her where nothing is hidden. She lies inside, expecting a message, though receives no signal until meaning's caught, pours out black, or is it lemon?

Who happens out the mammal room, next the throat, then the attic where it's warm and many sounds congregate. A whole course of thought before her in flesh, so she won't have to exist through words chosen to create her, confining her in creation. Maybe she'll remember right before death what's frightening, when the organization of our company changes light, at the point of vanish. Though there is no love at this moment, her hunger makes her aware.

Cistern

Forced forward toward space displaced from reason—the well, a hollow with exposure over and over subverts sequence and other order outside the unnarratable.

or if knowingly cut, the gnomon nomad measures locked light preceding its likeness without that unbridgeable gap—fishes pass echo not simply

can any knowledge be so young or too old or withdraw itself or water is temporarily removed till night appears ready, but what sort of coming is it if informed we have choice though are denied the right to turn back the dead

forgettable as a thought

Insoluble body was her past and time takes all tomorrows if you tock it up to the clock master who screws a rivet for a fence or the negative gate of separation

stake heart through oak rack

Disaster disappears in people doing its bidding and the sufferer has a liking for hot tears and mortal movement toward a new era, with relations mutilated, too cut to run and don't say don't go; the greatest place of hiding might be suicide, a see-saw is-was act where no one can return to squeal any answer makes the question possible:

or if Oedipus' swells were knowingly cut the gnomon nomad circuitously measures light locked into the shape preceding a set course he follows after its likeness, hence that nothing is without a doubt, the unbridgeable gap where fishes pass through gas like echo in order not simply to destroy but approach repose.

anyone makes the question speakable since the body he writes of as being a misleading link to danger or can he be disposed in a dram and the answer won't lack madness which is thought's guardian when wakeful,

save waves of sleep that watch over tacit surfeit in drift, and knowing becomes lighter at the hour edges of our parallelogram

other posited opposite site and part of the content is in too dark.

For one hundred years she slept under sea and in that deep the crashing blood against boat transpired, night was never longer belonging to her and how she fathomed

can sculpt new curves of thought but composition continues

After stars blow out the sky a smothering blanket of eight sights where no one knows an indiscretion in self torments torrents and overflows

loamy sediment and music make love made late in her life even ever after or look not at fallen mortals but the twins

who fell from the well immemorial wondered where smaller folk dwell, and imagine gravity the center of a secret harbored within the greater mass of self: ask, "When did I start?" "How do I awaken?"

The Still-Bound

Lay thee down the dwarf from under earth, a moon may climb the darkest side and we will reach in memory as chasms can. Divvied up, this fear annihilates shadows before what later will exist. We fail to dream but only what's believed.

She looks not through the clerestory window though sees something going out her eye while stain changes vision and she reacts with involuntary mind movements. Meaning extracted as light is caught between living and its look. She thinks farther than the traveling show, an imagining that soon as a new soul appears the last one is gaseous. And imagination: like genii from an inkwell, it cannot be drawn. Even there, walls break the earth into corners.

She could not live outside herself in a room she lets for sleep and to hold her in, but she is mostly aware of the terror, not how she found her way lying. There is a place of bodily grief. As long as it exists, mind cannot destruct, though it has to be as complicated as what's left under. If she detaches emotion from the external cause, one mistake contains more truth than another, the kind of analogies that exist between them. Errors played backward eradicate the previous from the new, and an object of regret ceases to be a passion when becoming an idea. She cannot recollect anything without obliterating the distinction between factual and conceptual sensations. Imagine what would happen if thought aroused emotion (o, that's right, it does) and the game won itself? The wind of the inward ear, sound off body; sometimes one can only believe where music leaves. It falls down from pain and the assignment of place. At the ocean she was warned not to break what others made.

Hole

Most households have a cave in back under the child or a building complex with beauty parlors that women enter midwinter, and when they return for the evening, their hair smells of sea and their flesh of fresh salt. The understory of a forest we splice open between words and memory, the gesture of mouth at f/8, eyes panning.

In her apartment, there is an empty space. She stands above the plot left for her in earth, looking down at her story. She knows what will happen. Between her self and her shadow. An outer space and inner place. He jokes about losing vegetables in her. And fruit trees. There is a garden, she disappears into it; where no shadows exist she forgets.

To open the earth costs, reaching depths of glaciation—twenty-thousand-year-old crystals hidden in under-air no body has touched. The last impressions pressed up against her, stored in earth like a memory candle. She knows rational destruction, an eruption, her thoughts projected against specter, across a cross of night. It's her mind she's not familiar with, yet.

By its nature, it is not in print. She tries to remember it on her tongue. The concept *circle* has nothing to do with language, neither do switches, inverted image of her mirror memory stored safely from children. Even the child in her self will never reach that high, carrying a piggyback shadow or voluntary prisoner. She crosses a body, of water, the warder of the brain. Will she find its absence in time? Shutting out the space where woods come from, burning to clear room, I can testify to its melt.

It exists as color forms. We know where it's from, the subaqueous, right between the surface. When she exits from love, her eyes create light projected onto skins, the way you spot death, catching sight of flight across the eyes. There were no flowers to pick so she picked bones to offer up to space; she tends to build inward, must be abided, but she can always construct or dismantle, or a man can do it for her; join all lines—a verticality never attained.

As soon as one settles on a planet. Action. We catch up to our cells carrying a portable kit of images, useful maps. She looks inside but doesn't know where the solution is, on a whiteboard perhaps. Walking into past mind, the battle over her memory. Who wins? Who keeps its most important moments? She gets custody of the child. The man of the house and car? He can drive away to strange parts. It's light in this hole. Each sun rising is that much different, or she is that much different after each night. Scream. It goes back to a wish.

Storm

> "As a child I lived in a small town. We always have a full moon. Every night, after dinner, my friend and I gathered 'round the backyard to play. My favorite game was to play with my shadow. We used to punch the shadow against the wall and set fire to it. Even though I was told my shadow would come to haunt me, I still did it. I did it to find out if my shadow had more strength than me."
> —Edelyne Gelin

Since the Big Doom Boom, we are but one sentence, internal yakking without pause—a keeper of gaze and an eye in fantasy or we wouldn't dream what is most fearsome: the presentiment that there must be a realm that assumes a self-contained sister system while I myself have found we are independent of one another; this I know as the object I am, and without truth-argument in common, we can be infinite and never cross the other's line, ignoring all words that aren't needed to assist our existence; yet if a union does occur, our multiplying thoughts will collide as imperatives in the midnight air, pouring out as open shadows, we wrestle in the vacuum of space between story and its penumbra.

Un

Her shadow she kept in seclusion, saw herself blind, until a voice said, *let it be that you shall see*, and He saw her, and she would not have to be the camera of herself. Mostly in dreams her eyes caught light when shut, and still He took notice—breast, vagina. Fog across the bathroom woman after storm; there is a reason, a scientific hypothesis for why first she sees nothing, then slowly the cloud dissipates to find parts bare before her and others gone. To be blinded means not to have eyes useless but to see something wrongly or to think you see one thing while an object from another dimension is before you. This she knows from her showers and can see as surely as God has sisters that He secludes with words, while He basks in sun and steam.

She ate clay tablets of Black Christ under streetlamps to understand possession is occupation of land. Of thirsty roots the size of spreading loins and singing trees, and beetles come to take song to their own time, to see the storm approaching, which wills no shadow.

During the total eclipse, she became impregnated with spirit and struggled with that demon brought inside by storm; thus, the idea of quality perceived is determined from motion or again as an arc of points, though not borrowed toward moon. The form invoked, involved in words, exists, as it is a reflected girl and therefore Nature. They clasp and twirl, gaining speed and loss, and no one falls; some fail because the corm has more strength than we can conceive

Sky Frames

Spires, geodesic domes, mirror-labyrinth, tractors, an Ethiopian lion, plastic human brain. She has an impression of it stepping out her head. "Journey 28, January: What water wants to weep me? Sleeping sorrow after sorrow."

How can she count an hour's past? if first must pass the half, then half again, never-reaching end. Whether water seems wonderful or not, she is prone to the dividing of extended substances. Molecular structures millions enlarged, sky frames, transistors. Hallucinations in time, there is no telling stone from space.

Numbers attained from the addition of thoughts. If one divides into many, are there more, or a faction? Small moves never calculated, wedged between the tragedies of nonexistent individuals violating extinction. In principle, it cannot occur, though the idea may exist. Nature of notions. What wants to be the monkey in the middle? The line between viscous and excessive.

Our most vicious part in unique architecture. Better to have one's fling in a small rooming house than an unidentified past. Time of removal is encroaching. Her pubic hairs dissolve after seventy divided by heart. It's a train line. Horizon. "Journey 29, January: Why can't I obey? I have gone back and hailed her out from death where I do not belong."

At noon she'd sneak from her room, order up hallucinations by serial. I spied her through (plot) (woods), glassed in a egac. She musicked off the boles. Ocean of emotions full, motion of moon, of light scales. Of scare. Full. "I am between my rememory. Each time it becomes more difficult. I touch Satan and know it is Satan. Though I am aware it may be satin. It may be you who can't be held like a body, not in mind."

The organic form establishes movement out of matter. Adam, a highly concentrated image of Mother. It was her whole fish she could not sever like reach from body: Can death and birth no longer function out of order? For all who looked down glass, did not object to this world lifting.

Absolutely

How far have you gone this evening or passed between remembrance other?

What makes it space, a trace-wound wound around her body with the notion there is something behind: A memory, a confused constellation, a white substance of which the heart cannot take the purity and cannot be conceived out of this world where her deepest errors steep suspended on gossip, and even if she stays awake, shift in placement occurs when air's gone astray or the spirit's sent off without flesh; for there is nothing so fearsome as no image, no thing to recognize we near.

In weather she is timid since last light finds a way down and turns away tidings. Always an absolute span as it curls out of her, withdraws, while snow accumulates, must mist over a moment of loss, and defection of passion is depicted by drowned river or heaving sea. If she were a bridge drawn between two spans of spirit, she'd be walked over.

Field of identity sustained, still part of the entire surface, a kind of thought that walks through her into a snowy field; she is all but a ghost, and he can talk freely about matters outside her. The more she fades into the woods, the sharper her outline and dimmer her concupiscent flesh. The words spoken about home automatically enclose under the roof or are framed by windows while she is climbing a tree and can be sought pointing to what isn't known. Into the recess she freezes needles, needs breath no longer, and footballs of small animals replace her, and she accepts this as the part of nature she'll never be a part of. Acts can be played in absence, and the world is that much changed without knowing why.

When done in a glow there might be an estuary that lay ahead.

Safe inside magma, the blind daughter and her brother with translucent skin feel no whether or which, just wet light lost to the clouds. With a telescope, she brings it into sight of escape, and who the devil also compels, pointing to the line from his heart and his private parts in the brain where we buried him so he could begin in a lone direction, canonized for emitting the most post-miracles, flesh-shed and supine. Each one masked, and she recognizes him in herselves—motion and sensation of sound in encamped concentration.

You try to remember where you became but with each step there is less trace to your past.

After he steps on her wrist, disturbing her intravascular volume, ocean closes up, though he can't cry in her high concentration of salt and peace. Anywhere is the same, and the distance between everywhere is not. Nor does the distinction between earthly and celestial become obsolete with the realization that what he sees or where he is could be other; the mutation of something into else makes self-evident identity is not a relationship between objects but between times. She could not be seen before he saw her, though nothing allows us to conclude ocular intelligence.

, and how this body relates to where it is or the bodies around it.

She is the wall of water from where she sees. Before her—a window on which is painted a solunar chart; behind her is devotion. Before her are bare trees; behind her, the world starts from what she imagines. She's not sure there are eyes on her wall, though wishes he were present to know the snow casting shadow melts into crests.

Though the sky arches and turns time around as she holds herself out for morning, names possibility, lurking to loom wonder in suspense.

When sketching, she takes the pose of her still-life study to understand, falls to her knees to feel the flame around him, and in charcoal, draws the ashes to her fingers. It is already simpler. She can turn any situation into pictures on paper. If she conceives a body as its movement, then something else exists that depends on her life and on greater, more complex bodies. She can't think of his name without changing shape. Across the way a friend is wiping with a photo of Ceausescu's blood.

Where spirits have an absolute exterior existence, where space with trimmings out of reach absolve her, but even if what she sees is not correct, there is sense in that we always conceive another who is greater yet never satisfied.

When you turned to follow your markings, the tread had all but been erased

After falling out of the forest, he forgets all secrets, forfeits earnings. He has memories of feelings, but one cannot hand over a promise of the sun with mauve strokes, the color of liver without delineation, and the inside of her. An amassing of images, of magic passes away and right or wrong fade from a bruise. One need only proximate experience; death flounders around skeletons, is attracted to light like the buzzing. When the Dutch door opens, you'll be able to answer most questions.

before you, a trace of what night might come to

Without warning her home became dangerous, tears from other parts of the train she traveled and observation intersected into infinity; it is the nature of scattered memory; it is the privilege of reentering renaissance and finding herself in his pockets of flesh; it is important to analyze how this particular feeling is composed and then dissociate all persons and things so it is only her own. The spectacle is doubly visible if her footprints are carried away and pulled into pieces as she bursts from east to west. The gaze disappears and they diminish.

and is trampled upon by an imprint that was once yours.

Looking through a window, one thing is sought and another seen, little to do with looking *at* the window. And she knows part of it is a secret and can't be said and that she is in him, breaking laughter, dangerously mixing aspects from one realm with another, so that some possibilities seem so plausible she passes over them without blinking an eye, while some bring her straight back into parts of herself she can't recognized nor know how they affect the body, only the feelings animated by the knowledge of things invisible.

Movement influences passion and property too, so the snow falling everywhere makes him an ocean away, though why the eyes bulge in space where there is little nothing to see has not been explicated, yet she believes it has to do with the theory she could ride light to his face and know him by reflection only. The soul has to be made desirable

It was once yours.

Coda

bellicose veins tattooed on the blue belly of your once most secret place, single linger still and linear

mouthflies hovering over, when the dying stops there are uncontrollable degrees of closeness

are we attached or involved?

deep down the manhole a hum or sung to someone in the sea
hear
seep

From Tales of Murasaki and Other Poems

Time Travel and Poetry

The following interview will take place in the middle of the night.
Punctuated by shakuhachi music and wind:

Lady Murasaki: Watching waterbirds on the lake increase in number.
Taking note of flowers. The way clouds travel season to season. The
Moon. Frost. Why would you purport to know the body of my land?
Carnal. "To know" in the most intimate sense. Through the senses.

Martine Bellen: Language represents a way of ratifying one's existence.
That the lover must absent himself for yearning, for desire, to occur. That
Writing embodies absence. "Shunyata. Form is exactly shunyata, shunyata
Exactly form."

Poetry probes what is heard when peering behind screens.
That which is known. Carnal. That which is closest to us.
Lady Murasaki, you are not known by your own name but by one derived
Of your father's title.

I am not mine.

When the Emperor makes an error
The world is set in turmoil.

When the poet sets pen to paper

Sets off on a journey

Begins to right it.

*

In the Heian period, writing in the Japanese language was private.
Men lost control of their language, women their bodies.

                                          Once a woman
Is known, she becomes a character in a romance that waits to be opened.
Carnal. She becomes poetry. We desire to know her and yet…

                             Words on a page or tracks across
Snow from a strange bird, indelible writing, melting writing. Strange
White bird that travels from snow to cloud. Poetry.

Inoue Mitsuo (author of *Space in Japanese Architecture*) writes that during Japan's feudal period (1573-1868), Japanese architecture allowed for the movement of space. Rooms of a home were not scattered randomly, nor were they organized geometrically. Space was discreetly revealed, revealed discreetly. Shunyata.

He compares movement-oriented Japanese architecture to episodic literature, such as *The Tale of Genji*.

What might happen when a girl walks out a door and begins talking. A home with rooms scattered randomly.

The way the lines of poetry slip past one another. Rooms connected by an elongated U or zigzagging corridors and natural sounds in negative space—rooms we open in to. Rooms that speak a foreign language. Rooms that write a different language than they speak.

Hayao Miyazaki's film *Howl's Moving Castle* sets Japanese aesthetics against a westernized landscape. A slippage in direction, meaning, syntax. The way a line might wander off and speak to a stranger. A spell might be cast. Powerful words that change the course of a life. Words originating from an older / other time. Older / other place. Words that have traveled far and long to meet you.

Terrifying Creatures

We met like bits of drifting duckweed

It is dawn and a woman lies in bed
with another woman's lover. His
costume, such glossy beaten silk that
one cannot tell if he is parting or a
part of mist and memory,
the path is endless

a cliff with water rushing down its face

———

if a bird flutters near flowers

if it flies into the candle's flame small as a bean

if it burns. if it burns.

Sitting on your floor playing with dolls.
Manipulating their arms, mouths, mating

If a bird cries for its mate, it can be consoled by placing a mirror before it. If a mother's blood is smeared on ancient coins, the currency will find her children, no matter how long it circulates. The biological system of love. We love to see the new straw moon spread across an absent sky. Night with a clear moon, a glass of clear water. We hurried to rise with the dew.

> Terrifying creatures with spindly arms and legs live on
> a sliding screen in a stormy sea.
> I open that screen, look into the eyes of a man who travels alone.

———

On the first day of the first month meanings become clear:

We dream my parents have sent a boat to fetch us. A messenger arrives at the house where we were born. When the guest feels he has seen everything, he takes a sudden turn or opens a door, and before him is a fence of plum trees and a wall with wandering vines. Troublesome ghosts and unhealthy objects such as ships arrive regularly, forcing their way into your most private place and scattering your furnishings; in between it looks to be a mountain, only there is no mountain. Nor any guest. Although this moment is spectacular we wouldn't want it to last a thousand years.

———

Our parting-fires, wild pinks. You apologize for having to go and for so long, halfway through our journey. Though one makes one's face look squished as if about to cry, it is no use, no tears will come.
> The noise of mosquitoes in my ear is thunderous, and I eat silver noodles to bring me luck, to lead me to you.

Dear old lover,

The reverse of a door has shut. You are no longer behind everything.
Soon there will not be any more pain because of you

How I imagine death to be

Letting go and slipping past. Shipping away.

Architectures

I

    Above you (at your coronation) stands the coroner.
        When you are not,
        Things are not
        As they are either.
        Ether through ears
        Rarefied radiant energy!

            What's more eternal than a falsity?

                Where the body is an appendix of the mind

II

                (control is had
                    in vast areas:
    meadows for sheep, urban centers)

    Your asafetida bag,
    Its rank, sacred emissions
    Ring around the heart

III

There we exchange prophecies, harmonies:

>Only they know
>Nothing is secret
>Being shapes
>However everlasting

Not since ancient Pindar or Maha Kashyapa had such space been rendered

Not since Pindar

Pillars of salt, vanishing vaults

The Knee

is part of the thigh of one who sits
crux of a hill or bowing grass
oiled knees, a supplicant
receiving blessing in the form of carpal articulation
or a protective coat around banes
where Spirit abides
a hemispherical route to god's
protective hollow

The Cat

A structure closest to light
                          Alert

Each ear composed
                    Of four octaves and twelve muscles

Circulate
        Ting sound

Flats and sharp
            Claws

                        Extensive communication

Nei Monggu

Hohhot, the Green City,
an autonomous region founded by Genghis Khan,
1000 meters above the sea,
Where stands silver Buddha flanked by musical instruments
Which the wind, snow, the sandstorms—
Plentiful throughout the spring—have mastered.
Here you can travel out of sleep
Aside trains of camel with grandmother's eyes,
Eyes once worn by all Mongolians

Who presently have wandered
To more hospitable regions, such as Junshang
Island, with its 72 gentle hills,
Its paradise of brooks, flowers, wild boor, and monkey,
As compared to northern terrain with grassland yurts.
Start at Hohhot, have a plate of mutton,
A camel hoof, a kabob, then follow, follow
The nomadic Mongolian road; it will deepen your life.

The Passion Of Martyrs

How time eliminates
Bone and hair

mosaic icons
stigmata weeping blood

Storks fill skies
Teeth crumble. An empire

maudlin Marys

lie. there's no image

Moves in a world of mystery
Not nuclear composition

sun-scorched cross

she spun thread

      Addicted to building
      Fortresses. Cathedrals

strung rosary beads

                            of gem and glass

        Form(s)
     in which pain
     is expressed

Ides/Ideas

On the eighth day after the vernal nones,
It fires—a Species or Nature,
Analogous to the paradigm
Scribbled in Beethoven's sketch-books
Or the first cupola constructed—a framing moment.

Arising from the salts left on the body,
Extracted from its ashes, the image,
Phantom, the attribute, figure
of speech, the vespers, whisper purple-martin, whisper.

House
(Home)

Houses know everything about everything.
When they are themselves, it does not matter
How people treat them.

Homes know everything about everything when they are themselves.

Windows especially are treated because through windows
Others know everything about everything,
How people treat themselves in houses.

Houses which know everything about themselves are themselves a part of everything.

Screens know little about concealment.
When they are themselves, screams
Enter or exit.

Screens know everything about divisiveness.

Homes know people,
Know their skin, their eyes,
Themselves.

Snails' homes are made of calcium or human nails.

Homes that live in people. People who carry knapsacks
Or passports to the *bodega*. People who are houses,
When they are themselves, they know everything about everything.

IV

The city walls were eyelids.
A worried prayer rug,
Honeyed saffron and crimson designed.
The white bird offered its *corazón*
To your black cat who rubbed and licked
In an attempt to ease a remarkable hole.

V

Your reflection in a shard
Formed by ancient hands

Dust of a past desire
Traces and signatures.

WHAT THE ANIMALS TOLD

Fortune was round, fast, waited for no one and supped on mice. It never stopped being magic, not quite green but it created a before, a bus stop. Sun had no teeth, moon was filled with them; when her mouth was an opening, I would walk in for protection. It is the spirit who takes us to our birth, has separated land from air. Mother partook in the beatings though feigned innocence. Nothing so tame as a drum but a fiery pony—the meeting of lightning and Earth, the wheel and what it can do. Instinct is why we wore rabbit-ear necklaces. asking for a name. a husband. a home. We know what the animals do because we married them. At night they scurry up our bodies, take flight in us. Rob our fruits, vow their love, fill votive jars with strange and smelly substance. At night they steal us from our men and take us on space ships. They speak the future and we understand better than we would have thought. They give us children that we eat as protein. We take the love in our laps and plant it. We plant our future dinners. We plant them in us.

Let door and bolt know I am under the protection of Coatlicue

Slaves and artists are sacrificed as their flesh matters least but their souls suffer most. The blade was black, obsidian, eclipsed light. Lift your palms to check they bear no weight and pray if he asks you turn from your mother—she wears a necklace of hands and hearts while her hands are serpent heads—cannot carry—and her heart is eagle claws, cannot feel. At her base is the Flower Man or Poet, his heart so open he is near a flower himself and his ears plugged with jade—

    A wand held to her mouth,
magic anticipated, incantation.

Let door and bolt know I am under the protection of Coatlicue

As in all markets there are many mangy dogs with tooth necklaces bordering their half-dead souls. You mouth a word and small gods, dressed as urchins, beg the gold that you cannot pass up, cannot part with. Like Coatlicue, the hands cannot hold but flag by your side, a reminder and disclaimer.

A little white dog—purity of the soul—sits by your feet during meals, offers help. Feed him and you'll have a friend for life.

———

I caught fish from your mouth, deboned and fried in quasars, what makes it *quasar* is its voluminous dark side. Then we snuck a secret and fell into sleep. His arms were big, and he was ashamed of them. I carried a lamp and peeked into each window, calling out the time. This is your memory too, a community meal for all to partake; you added a few of the details and sat back to enjoy. Dead sailors brought messages in a treasure chest; though I can't read them, they open onto copious bounty.

Coatlicue rubbed her serpent against the flowers, hoping to secure them, but the serpent would wrap tight and break their attachment to Earth.

———

when she awakens, she realizes something not known before sleep, awakens full, ate much over the course of the night. Nine course meal in a dream, blood courses through with spirit

in dreams, all vehicles are available yet none are needed

Women don't travel alone. People who sit together speak the same language. It is easier to understand than to speak. Understanding might not seem like enough. Understanding might be plenty.

Its color forms content, spirit. . .not whether it's a quadrangle, blanket, warms you, but that it is yellow and screams "Ohhh!!!" when you enter the room (dream). falling into a hidden pass called *allende* (beyond). In the far reach is a bookstore filled with spells and needs; beyond that, a cluster of tables and chairs used to rest and take your coffee. There's a billboard advertising Maria Lloroso Pasado; for 5,000 pesos she will tell stories of the erotic, of far off fairies, other lands and legends. For another 3,000 she will read your palm, the stars, she will feel your ovaries, darn your socks, drive you to Rio and then home. She will speak your tongue

———

Your Reverence,

Firecrackers light the dawn while saints dress. A ballgame's in progress. Our sleep takes a station break. Don't know what side I'm on. It is not for us to see but to hear. Our parents are making us. Love. Soon the sun will rise. We will be born. Pamphlets distributed in a sea-creature language.

Small parades scatter about the streets. Parallel and perpendicular. Sometimes they merge, sometimes disperse. Like the amebas in our bellies. A brass band follows devils and tarts of the church who dress as Christ and mime drinking and philandering. A young girl wears a loincloth and spreads at the cross. She is looking inside herself.

Jaguar swallows a rooster, which represents the sun. Another day eaten.

My God has forsaken me and vanished

———

Out of her mouth came streams of stone; it is a door too, the tongue a lock and key. *Puerta*. Portal. Pearly Gate. Her teeth were white though one was missing.

It is darkness who wraps her legs around Earth and rotates. Darkness meaning everywhere looks of fallen snow. Meaning open eyes unsee. Blindness because what's in front of you isn't in front of most others. Because you *see* darkness. Blindness because you think you know yourself better than your acquaintances, while they know you better than your friends. Isis weaved her eyes and ours; that can be crooked but also comforting

Blood from the mouth snaked into the ground. words which you tasted, salty and with iron, that strengthened them and, through them, you.

———

May the Goddess who has abandoned me show mercy

6/23/00

Last night the light broke the sky to mate with Coatlicue who, from her depths, expounded in a language with which I'm not familiar, from a time when words were not representations but were themselves objects of desire, when fire, *fuego*, cousin of wind, was not a proper schoolgirl who politely asks for a glass of water, but a dynamo who scorches the Earth of its plunder.

Listening to mother in her quarters crying, experiencing a passion I have known only in dreams. I spell out my feelings in my notebook; they become distant from me in the writing, a howl escaping from its spot of origin and now, unattached, it is un-understandable, an abstraction outside of its time.

reshape walls. will. what structure isn't/what life hasn't

———

Fry up the sky, tortilla grilled in oil or thyme, our stars slight green as toads toes; Three Jaguar eats sun with moon topping. She thought she was going to dinner but ended up being it. Two Husband said she was instilled with a labyrinthine amount of self-worth and not one deferring bone in her body. The handsome doctor took x-rays, said none are broken. She recognized *inside* the best, the structure, the stone. Foundation holds us and is humanity, needs excavation and renovation. She read *The Book of the Dead* in different translations, at different times of night. To get it right.

Last Will: Things to leave behind—Mesoamerican mask, my identity. I have brothers, sisters, am part of a family, am part of two, am part of none. What I brought: some clothes and makeup, mascara. What I'm returning with: a whistle for the moon to follow, pen disguised as an Aztec sacrifice knife, and if I'm lucky, maybe some change. What I'll be returning to—? ? ?
Lost: telephone privileges, a history, my language. And gained: a sprain. spleen. stone soup.

———

With one cup of light left in the sky, night rests on the lap of dreaming bear. I create with him when there is no place to go. After all, who isn't fearful of sleep where not even dreams can manage a way in. The fisherman sits at the troller's edge and sinks his line in the clarity of water. Graves are made in the wake, but with so much transparency comes depth and in death darkness, so still, as the scribe working aside memory, in the process, loses much of her own

———

In one visitation I am made of sky. Coatlicue wants her past in me so she studies tense to teach her what to do. It is a preponderance of swallows, fly down the throat and into the closet of the mouth and where that might lead. In her the gods are drunk on heart, I pass as thought

Let door and bolt know I am under the protection of Coatlicue

Space does not hold our travel. She would listen only to the sounds she put there. Corn is sacred because they are ears and yellow with drops of blood. She wants for the rooster to bring in the day, with heat and his wife, his tongue scaled as a serpent's

―――

5/23/00

Because of retrograde, what is moving forward will look backwards so do the opposite. Be the opposite of what others think of you. Forget ideas, ideals, tests, torts, morals, murals. Directions aren't your forte, so give up your north. And when you feel most lost and scared, you'll find the dirt road that you're looking for. *Love* is too general a word, like *Democracy* and *Truth*. Yours and others. He would not let you into the bookstore because he thought you a thief, that you had it in your heart to lift Rimbaud. If a man puts his arms around you, look into his ear. If his heart is clean. If he's familiar with love, too familiar. If you know his name, call it as a spell into him hide and change.

Tales of Murasaki

Dream Of The Spider Bridge

I

Because she found darkness in the recesses of home most frightening
Because clouds traced sad lines across the sky
She put out to sea

> Careful to choose lucky days for our beginnings
> The honeyed moon, two nights past full

> One envies waves that must return whence they came
>   and rows them to avoid tangles

> "…even the skies have closed down

> "even the mind has gone
> against invertebrate habits"

The boat hiding inside a depression, a brushed tear induced by the splashing of our oars and calls of overhead geese, wild and barely visible, not storied to be otherwise

"I caught the ferry
where I never caught it before

"Mother was with me holding hand to heart but so severely I thought of alligators known to eat their young and other cold things. The sky was darkening and I asked him if perhaps this was an omen and we should set out in another way but spoke so quietly because he seemed particularly rough and as changing as the sky that threatened rain. Many fears ran through the whole of me; I wanted him to stop, tensed my limbs, my voice left first…"

"It was dawn inside
when I made ready to leave"

II

Too long a winter's day to make way through these snows where uncommonly elegant fishers dwell and rustics who could not identify the music were lured out into sea-winds there to catch their death.

"I will take to you
a bottle of Soju and fried fish"

An old woman whose only remaining task was to die brought to the temple, as an offering for a better position, a Chinese coxcomb box. A man who did not recognize her came into her dream. In it, an enormous passage of time was created and two players took and untook the same stones for all eternity without affecting the larger disposition of forces. It can be set up as a game and the desired results can be attained and yet, at the moment when the situation looks as it had been foretold, the ten directions appear altered and even now the result is at a distance. These never-tended gardens covering foxes and owls howling in unpruned groves morning into night.

She had been closer than she ever deserved or knew

III

    we should not allow it such a hold on us

IV

Her hair collected as it fell

bamboo

ten feet long stuffed in incense jars and test tubes

sowed herbs

what is left, after, or the worn path inside

wormwood

"And I had thought then that I was unhappy; it is no better now"

Fifth Day of the Fifth Month (the most propitious)

Mother said in the big book all is written and so I began my own small one with myself as a peripheral character to trick I wrote it on azure rice paper and with my left hand. I chose words by others rather than my own. Mother, I ask, are you referring to predestination? Is there nothing I can do with only the day of death important enough to be marked? So many numbers writes god the mathematician, keeper of deeds and destruction. Abacus and rosary. She binds my fingers and toes in tape and bleeds me. I am your mother and must prepare for it, my duty to keep you small and in order.

V

peepers and glass frogs. It was a moment of recognition, when the scene changes and we realize reversals. That is what makes for tragedy. Flip-flop of the magnetic field. It can be tracked. If A = B then who am I?

I love to watch you
    the way you position your workman hands and dig through my nipples
        the color, for example, is dried red
            my star looks grape, a finch dressed in raspberry sauce

the day you position your hips

your back becomes the walking night away nothing becomes you better

The falconer offered a sampling of his take. Everything he brings together in himself for me to receive but he cannot dream truth and it is that which ties with ribbons this world to the other. A Judas tree grows on the moon. It sheds shadows and he calls me traitor. Letters filled with warm vowels; I return avowals. He knows better than most what a mistake it is to get attached to a place or trust a life that is not ours to trust. I write by firefly. It is the mating call, the need for more. I never came away without some small thing that seemed precious, touching things, annoying things.

She seemed in danger of falling in love

In her garden, however, was not the smallest suggestion of disorder:

Yellow yamabuki reflected
on the pond as if about to join
its own image. Moon passed moss
carpet. Abeyance beneath
a star-filled bowl, jewels worn
by the Pleiades

Bringer of Light

VI

They looked for her where they thought she might be.

I made no move myself to try the river for the black cloud boiled overhead and sonorous strains of royal deer scattered about the forest where red silks were beaten to a soft luster and gossamer of delicate saffron stirred in waters once expected to find a muddy mood floating upon it one found a bright yellow. Also, dew collected on her evening face she had so briefly to find a passage over a thousand years.

Beauty and pain had come to appear much alike.

———

Tale Of The Ancient Princess

I

Moaning of prayers in morning air.

   The world cast inside a cicada cage made of bamboo.

   In search of a nunciary—overtones echo home.

   Cloud echoes cloud,
         clouds break like bread and steam rises
                into the stream that flows through a stupa.

She no longer welcomed
familiar spirits who left messages
in layers of dust and in motes, their bon mots

   Wild grasses strangled the tamed. Bindweed barred corners.

                      The garden she inherited had been taken
                        by numerous apparitions, number less,
                           numbing, and humming autumn

   "Left alone in those warm rains
   her hair would grow dank"

II

    Her self is never
        recognized but represented
            impermanently and movement,
                another imitation.

Evening waves darkened   (Those constant travelers
the Lavender Princess's sleeves.   crash against cliffs,
foaming,
                                            and reforming

boulders by their tales)

She had grown taller, more beautiful
from the gathering of far-off sights.

Now that the past is done, it stands
        before us as though it were today.

Nor would she remember to bring it wrapped in rice paper to the meadow.
Always elusive as daylilies,

Oh! what a sad plight, lost amid dream, shaking, shaking.

How does one exit such a story?
Stay with us a while and maybe
the situation will look different.

Fireflies And Summer Rain

I

It is the Sixth Month and Malevolent Gods
are concealed under her goose feather pillow.

She will not be one of those unfortunates
who lives too long (always the adolescent dreams

of a short life) but will form into the whirring of wings
or dew on shallow eaves or the privacy a young girl requires.

In the old stories, the Lavender Princess took courage.
Her low spirits

> "Guided by the moon
> An errant spirit"

And air warmed from the stirrings of martin bells.

> Dewflower, Dragonflower
> May-beetle, Tigerbeetle

Certain *dei* lead from this world to the next.

                          A strain on the koto. The hollow
                          of her clavicle impressed
                          by the closeness of music,

its spider web

                          of sound, invisible and captivating

The devil's rival:
Field Music

Tomorrow she will forget how enamored she was, taken by
                                  the concert of chirrups
and peaking blooms.

(sounds music words)

Monkey music

III

She, the Lavender Princess, hidden behind a screen
               so the young prince could allude to her

scent and shadow.

He, not allowed the briefest glimpse during his diurnal
                amusements, amassed paintings of brilliant

color to excite sense.

In her pillow book she writes:
       Good days, bad days—simple days,
       Morning & night—more days.
       Regard the light! How it projects
       a visual voice of Buddha, and bouquets
       of breath rise off wild grasses,
       like Bodhisattvas.

      We are not forgotten.
An omen

Early Autumn Whispers

I

"Girls are so beautiful," she says, as she outlines my
shoulder with her eye, and my arm becomes an object,
something for me to touch, admire, remove.

Something I could not object to.

        Residue evaporates

        its ghosting shape

        over my gross

        shape

II

    Locust's shell

    lies in my heart

    forbidden center or dialectic

    as between wind and cottage,

    home, and hill that surrounds home.

—exists possibility
and exits

moon surfaces
sun, sortie

dimmed lamp
think of less

forget
the gate.

III

Banished for past wrongs

and assigned a task

which one is unaware

of attaining

in containment.

She tangles wool into sweaters.

I wear her designs. It is fall, colder,

and paths are leaf-strewn

I believe in her power, earnest fate

and illusion.

IV

Accepting parts of oneself one would rather not

Expecting

another to be part of one

like surviving fragments, descendants

of the mountain that have broken off

uncertain shores and same waters

prepare for a union. Forms of recurrence

Reprise Dream

She says she is leaving me

but I hear, "I am leading you"

and follow.

From The Vulnerability of Order

Perrenials

First aria
In open field

Bulbs bloom, come crocus,
Nexus viola, trillium

Look to the bow and lyre
How opposing forces agree

Moon poppies backdrop
A carpet of columbine

Symphytum spoon spread
Red in bed of pink then cream

Variegate color and bass
Ah, the blues, the *blues*.

Cuccina

I

The most beautiful order is still
A random collection
Of things insignificant in themselves:

II

Cranberry rosettes and candied
Violets, frosted thumb plums
Sweating midday, and gingerbread
Shaped in stars and bells.

III

A buck, doe, and fawn dunk
Apples down near the pond where
Blue heron stalks rainbows
That dart while light recedes.

IV

Under feather comforters and tea-rose vaults,
We sleep smelling of last night's
Spices. Outside, trees shed quilted leaves.

White Butterfly

If every butterfly were smoke, would all perception
Fall to smell? If every wing were paper-white, would

All perception end in sight?
Stitch of Michelin lace or brood of Phoebus Parnassian.

This subarctic gossamer,
Kaleidoscopic absence absorbs alpine stonecrop

Across sage flats
Tundra

And bleeding
Hearts. She escapes the loose cocoon

In grass tussocks which protect.
And evaporates before a gust.

Swifts and Swallows

Sparrow-sized swallows swoop
Insects, peck bayberries. An aberrant
Of notes and dives. Though an incomplete

Breastband may confuse a tree
Swallow with a rough-winged one,
The voice, *weet, trit weet,*

Not a harsh *trrit*, rougher
Than the bank swallow's *trr-tri-tri,*
Should clarify. For those who wish to know the world

Must learn it from its detail.
Its swallowlike swifts, with illusory wing,
Alter a twinkle and glide.

All Beasts Are Driven to Pasture

Buddha Bear, sea lion on surface, sleeps in the sink,
Slinks under city drainpipes. But weekends allay

Hibernation of the vestigial tiger, and the Buddha
Rubs snout to grass, limb extends limb. Stalks

Deer and wild turkey. Devours flying dragons.
Bottled in muscle for flight, my beast chases bee up a tree.

The Vulnerability of Order

for Elaine Equi

Caves, here, contain dead / live
snakes some keys, for instance,
have holes or   ,
the transgressive guardian, mind
with wings beneath.

She felt the urge to send musk-confects,
Across the Strait of Gibraltar

Interior, private floods, neshamah (Jewish soul),
food with cinnamon curry,

Here, sea-goddess hosts aquatic monsters,
Traipse rabble of spooks
& devil's marionette. She attends lectures on anatomy,

Explores the yolk sac, our centerpiece,
Primitive heart. *Her*

Secret breath sounds the confident demons
Attune
      atonement
            a vowel an opening to the divine

God resides in the odd
Clamor, the *Ein Sof*

Female indwelling (pre-séance)
Oldest mystery of my ear
Opening the door   *shutters*   where message is married

Wind between heaven &   , word & lip
     Lived both forward and compassion *om mani padme hum*
How moment follows movement

She is *bemidbar* or in the desert
With *bubbe meise* (a grandmother's tale)
Law without vowel
Roofing planet-strooken

   For this woman, paralyzed and word-full,
   Chained to a mobile home with its process narrative,
   God is the one who counts
   Numbers, days, seductions, bones

   Inscribed in body. Outside
   She's drowning, weeping,
   Will stop at nothing for time.

Her voice, the wandering part of her
Flesh, in the Old / New Synagogue
                    In parchment, in hieroglyph.

Nocturne

Swan sails a milky tide, spread evenly across Silver River
& Pierrette, angry with the moon and universe of flute, viola,
harp, harmonizing our corrupt selves with the utterly impassible
Unable to suffer
Without leitmotiv

    Not to denote absence but to describe in negative
    terms, to capture the fades and sequences

The equation—peering at the sky upside down, at Cassiopeia,
    A sequin,
        Butterfly's dream, Andromeda
                Philosophical toys
                      Contenting emblematic identity

Below her waist: blue coral

    Cloud's breath root-coiled to earth
    How matter's faithless

    Miscellaneity under a simmering cinder moon
    Omen of bones, ignoble, central moods

    Crinkum-crankum frogs congesting trees,
    Shaded by a turbid glow

Bee's familiarities
With the wild moon.

Key to the bright world

Communal & personal aspects of integrating with sound as landscape
    (*converted luminosity*)

She sleeps in black-and-white woods,
Only when awake do colors saturate
Habitats of resonance
Glass splashed with spells, *canciones*

Ghouls, fouler wind, and swollen waves
                  A passing moon, passion moon

        The sword, which lies ready for battle in the open heart, shiny moon
       (A hidden moon scuds behind broken cloud)

Or is the Divine Window—apprehension of our invisible body
Tucked away in the prose closet
Neck-ruffles of stars and the *dones d'aigo*
Sheltered in underground waterfalled halls, weaving water
To gowns, the living mutable spirit of each fountain:
        The Tender Fount, Coarse Spring,
          Spring of Deceit, Glassy Fountain,
               The Dried-up Spring
(*reduce amount of blood in body, reduce desire*)

Innermost subtle drops
                Suffusing throat, heart

Gave speech to bird and wind
That dance for an audience of one; still swirls
Of bejeweled tulle pirouette in echoing applause,
Like the clinks of cordial glasses
Inspiriting the dark alone

She is an idiot, walks through the burden
Forgetting what disappeared. Her
                World fell away. A wind, hitherto unknown,
              physically unanimous,

All the Devils of Hell cannot pluck a feather from one poor wren.

Magic Musée

for Joseph Cornell

I

She, who's overconscious of her cage
Formed from heat, moisture, frost, concealment,

How it drips, freezes, fogs,
How it forms columnar cracks gashed with glass

Toward the blue peninsula
The visible half of reflection

Attempting to sense the solidity of an object

Or to remove the clothing of sound,
Disrobing at the Hotel Eden

Inventing a way in
To that which is built over concept.

II

Behold, Thoreau sings for owls; Dickinson, hummingbirds
Still life frames world of spectacle

Or object-spirits

Dewish   mute

The Pyramids are letters;
Cul-de-sac feelings; or Stonehenge, numbers.
In twilight the lamp illumines ideological will.

III

A weaving of walls, wicker
& caravan carpets strung twixt reeds.
Our ground breathes, floats, as we wander
Into cosmologies, cosmogonies,
Immeasurable emblems of circumference.

III

She developed the disease of demonic enthusiasm
On looking at a nymph.
Mystic hunt through childhood, *histoire* of fountains
Dominating the *jardin*   canary parasols
Perpetual noon   antipasto sun   *créme* ballerina
Idyllic dying swan.

IV

Wire-netted cage papered with constellations
Promises of origami flight from her magic prison
She traces an analemma, her eyes
Map the night sky or soap bubbles
Navigated by songbird
Whose droppings streak the air—
Reminiscent of a comet's tail,
The result of yesterday's path-strewn birdcrumbs.

V

Occupants of the *Étrangers*
Exalted chanters with a self-contained view
Small white frame

Moon
Sustained patterns of meaning

Spindly-armed shadows stretch through lace curtains
Unraveling the mind's voyage

As with other repressions, a vestige of the animal within
Or a continuum of the borderland known as *Nostalgia*

Her liquid limbs spider dance to melody
Foaming grottoes & feathered lures

Travelogue of a faun's dream.

Devi

Turn back, return
one thousand years, twist
her curved back, carved sandal-
wood hips, till time takes her

      subtle body between states achieved by accelerated deaths

into the Dance of Kali.
Space shivers. Siva. Was his face
blue? or did her eyes catch
the ocean in a filament of rippling skin?

———

      The sky, no longer beyond our grasp but an interior composition,

with color, too   foam
and many preservers—Vishnu, Parvati, Durga

foreboding as any keep, craving, enchanted weapon

———

Pelicans, flamingos, herons—the *mantig a tayr* (language of birds)
language of escape. An elegy is the bond between air and breach,
                          a released energy
the loosed verve of devotion

The hidhid,

      A tree gracious enough to lend its name to the mountain that houses its roots

      Wind that scuttles leaves is an elegy
      Birdsong: an elegy
      Ring of holy chants

———

      Devotion: repeating a practice without repetition,
              devotee,
                     Devi,
                            votive

A fifth world war fought outside time
Mind part battlefield:

Unborn   enduring   indestructible   embodied   inspirit

What dissolve are the ordinary aspects—
The ghosting roots of an ash,
    A butter-lamp,
        Intestinal garlands,
   Lands that lack volume.

This is autumn

Smells of sun and mums rise from spindly grass

If matter and energy are equivalent and light
the manifestation falls between,

Space between her teeth
                She sings scales

A breeze gathers synergy

Said to affect the Pacific Ocean, (specific) opens her mouth

Universe of names

Elegies for indigo and saffron leaves,
rain pounding rock. Reedy notes immerse
lichen, all variety of fern and fearful creature.

Look! Two birds in the tree, one eats, the other regardeth only.

A last scream lingers like the mocking of brilliance
from an extinguished star she prays
on. Midnight breeze caresses her.
(She cannot dance it, laden with apples,
popsicles, obstacles.) Her spine
visited by Shakti
                from the forehead of Durga

her most terrible aspect,

circling the throat and sex
with Kiki's glass sperms, skulls, with fury.

No rationale for this natya
of shattered aura, shattered faith

    Sadhana   (practice) forges the heart
        the jiva and atman. One bird eats; the other, a witness

    dresses of Prada scarves of Chanel

———

Where Sound corresponds to creation,
Hear Great Vac's drum, the goose lives
In the Himalayan's shadow, pilgrim soul
Takes flight toward columns of continuum—
Composed of sand, saffron threads, unexcelled
Wisdom, wind or mirrors,
    Our protective circles

    Oceanic volcano throat
    Opens a world disturbs
    The deep prana

Scarves of rustling light

Foundation Mandala

for Claire

Of sapphire. Systematically construed
off a square; offering
deities a balcony on which to dance

How does one illuminate the atmosphere?

Sheath of candles
Irrigate the four winds

Ganesa 'round back repairs walls
while the girl maps elements of philosophy
and posthumously eavesdrops on Grandmother,
whose files, over six-feet thick,
contain wisdom applicable to Vermeer, birds, *fabula*,
penny arcades, and the chance encounter
of a sirocco and softened laughter.

The girl, disguising herself as an old spider
In a thirteenth-century liminal magic lantern,
exacts impulses from light and pearls of moisture
that accumulate on complex webbing
as Picasso eats cats,
woos & plays the flute.

This boundless structure, binding structure,
city of flesh and bones

Hear white wheat
where mind drops, a vibrant precipice.

Indra inspects the floors of the building,
consults diagrams drawn in mineral on brocade,
tests supports, balance, flexibility.

Holiness as a star,
      octagon, circle, jewel

      Traditionally sand-painters applied this city
      of shadows, channels culs-de-sac,
      moving inward toward its heart

Trappings in Grandma's cabinets
the girl uses to construct conditions of weather,
directional colors, the need to escape; she pirouettes
atop the head of a pin, petals of tears and pomegranate
minaret. My lost ballerina sloshes ringside the spectral
world held in place by neural wind where everyone
has two names, lives according to the outer universe
or train's harmonic connection to its crossing

*drywall, five transparent layers
of panisks, dakini, guardian dragons*

Consecration of this mandala eliminates reversals—
a frameless forest from throat to heart
in ornamental buildings, with indelible
arms to carry and heal when embraced.

Tinkling bells announce transition of natural phenomenon

Belle Starr

Belle, wake up
Her cheek resting on the icy pond

Shadow of a thug turkey-shot her in the back, neck, and breast
Colt tore through her face

Her last bath in turpentine and crimson cinnamon
Pallbearers dangle six-shooters

Corn bread in the coffin
Wake up, Belle

On the other side the bread was ett
her outlaw in-laws provended.
A smile welds those wire lips
under wired lids—black
beaded eyes, a sky
on ceiling tacked, another world.
Only it is opposite,
so when she dies here, she finds her hope,
hemp-rope holding all in place
with peckish ravens darting back and forth.

Father was an innkeeper. We called him
Judge for his sternness and popularity.

(He locked her in
his closet, to keep her
his Confederate virago.)

A wingbeat

the haunts the hurts, ball and chain.

In dream you crackle like ice over earth,
like lust against the plains.

As a child, to harbor a secret
lands you in bondage;
then, as a woman, outlaws
harbor in your heart and land

Belle a born uglee

Eyes evolved not
because of mind's need to see—
but neurons must preexist
with a light sensitivitee

———

                Cherokee sun is she

Down Dallas way she's
The Bandit Queen,
Queen of the Outlaws,
Long velvet train
Riding her stallion Black Venus
Down the main

Fare table, whiskey up, and those
Jolly lads, southern nightriders

While Jim was out, a scout
For the next crime scene

Nesters, squatters, shooters
Who'd disarm or arrest her?

Who'd undress her?
A .45 under her skirt.

Word has it the Tumbleweed Wagon rolls
and gangs travel, wheat in the wind.
The iron-rimmed-wheel prison
wields fear from afar where humans
like hounds armed to the teeth
are shackled in irons and washing
the dishes and fighting
fires that burn through the prairies.

When Belle and Sam Starr were apprehended
on a horse-stealing charge, she tossed out
the blankets, the pots and the pork,
the stove, and the fork. So the marshal tossed
Belle on the cold metal floor with rebuke.

That year, she fixed 'em a grand supper of rattlesnake stew.
And coffee like glue.

Rolled on the floor as they puked.

Yes, the Petticoat of the Plains, dare-may-care. She rolled
on the floor as they puked. Thus, outlaws sought her advice.

She, their Guiding Spirit, gave chase
In black invisible

Wound in a buckskin
Of rattlesnake rattlers

Up north the Hi-Early Mountains
Far west a cranberry sunset
The earth on Cherokee Nation

Only approach to her cabin
Was through a narrow canyon

Fortlike with fine furniture
Famed for its Hawkins' Portable Grand,
And its Belle Starr Creek

She washed her feet and raised
Her girl Pearl to be a lady

Coarser variations of air produce sound
Stillwater Penitentiary
Released on bond and a shopping spree

Each husband shot, replaced

She could read the wanted posters
On each face

Their obituaries
She could read

———

With the grace of a cat
the Colt left his holster

Velvet sky
Moon on high
Last star seen

Pocahontas

Too far away to be
Seen singly, they come

Together. The coat-wearing
People. They come

On floating isles. Carry
Thunder sticks. They look

For back seas where clove
And mulberry grow. They come

From beyond the great ocean.
With a cross God

They come.

Her first English word was "jewel."

As the sun rose, Ahone took the stream water
off her body and she was one, cool and sparkling.

Mocha brow. Wide-dipped fauna, mutant birds,
water monkeys, and other delights sketched in oyls

on her legs and arms. Maybe ten when she cartwheeled
past his men, proud of her strength, a wilde girl.

Bid Pokahontas bring hither   *Kehaten pohahontas patiaquagh*
two little Baskets, and I will   *ningh tanks manotyems*
give her white beads   *neer mowchick rawrenock audowgh.*
to make her a chaine.

    Hither she ran, and round
    her neck a circle of light

    Language and desire
    to understand magic

    the other possessed the other's
    country, a half each didn't know

This priest of paper   This stranger
conveyed truth   from nothing
when he sent a word   lives outside
without his body   ear

    Distance
    between
    as sea
    and land unite
    in the state of flesh

If not for the daughter
Who durst not be seene
Cheek-streaked
Trader

Hidden under
Heathen moon

Wilde traine
Berry juice and bloodroot
Through irksome woods
I will keep my promise
In exchange for some peeces, a cock, and hen

Love you not me?
Deep in Powhatan territory

Pocahontas:

Baptized Rebecca, the Lord Jesus
loves me, but at night, with shoes removed,

my toes still smell of our Algonkian ground,
and wise ancestors visit and whisper our secrets.

Small skins I leave for laughing Ahone
who tickles my soles. And though Father could not agree

to all their demands, they would have permitted
my return but soon I met John Rolfe,

farmer of the esteemed weed and, after moments,
realized I found the stranger in myself.

A marriage between two hemispheres.

Tomocomo:

Powhatan orders to know the number of men
   in this England, but many exist
      as leaves or grains of sand, too infinite
         to count. Here, soil abandons earth.
            These explorers of liquid-ground who sail air.

The Daughter in whalebone
   dresses as these people
      and so does her son, the next chief
         who will
            always smell
               a foreign beast, even to himself.

He will step atop a house, walk on their cloud.
   When I stepped off the *Treasurer*,
      onto Plymouth, my dreams
         shrank smaller than what they've created.

      I am diminished.

John Smith:

Eight years since we last met, and cry
she did upon seeing me whom she thought

dead. Worse behaved Christens
I have met. She nineteen, a mother,

colonist. God must have helped in her conversion,
like any young lady, upon the settee she sat.

    Yet all I had taught
    her and she me,
    how our hands felt, fell
    to our sides, as language failed.

Pocahontas, first Native American
to die on foreign soil. She left us
a son, inheritor of her
mother's land.

Calamity Jane

Here, the season of manifest destiny
And breaded trees

Land-hungry time
Backstairs time

In each of us
An eyewitness

Marthy Cannary
By herself

An eyewitness

———

Born 1852, Missouri
oldest of six brats

rider until I became an expert rider,
able to ride the not-ridable
horses, which I spent
my early and later life riding

overland to Virginia City, five-month
journey, hunting the plains
or adventuring, shooting
and riding way beyond

many times crossed
the Rockies
to Montana, our wagons
lowered over ledges,
boggy places, no use
to be careful

lost all, horses and all,
then there were dangers,
streams swollen; mounted
a pony to swim through currents and save

lives or to amuse ourselves.
Narrow escapes. Simple escapades,
reached for obstacles and overcame
as God is witness.

At Blackfoot, Mother died;
I buried her under the spring.
She taught me weather,
strength, and to cuss. Then

To Salt Lake. Where my father dies.
Joined General and his campaign.
Between Deadwood and Custer
Molested very little.

Ordered out to the Muscle Shell
Or Nursey Pursey Battle; in saddle
Swirled to catch and cradle
Egan in my arms. Christened
Me Calamity, heroine.

To rely on what
One had once
Lost faith

Perseverance keeping
The quiet outer
Fact

Synchronicity and spirit

Doris Day is Calamity sipping sarsaparilli

Bill can't see her beauty till she drops
her coat, can't see her
face or coif. Or hear her
sing, "My gun got so hot
had to sit with a muzzle between my legs."
Her magic: pink chiffon.

Made into a woman

"no changeless essence...no eternal verities"

Custer Custer elle était plus qu'une prostitutée
a true star of gold
orneé d'une étoile
la *défroque* of all *théatre*
tout le monde

Jane Russell and Jean Arthur,
John Wayne and Bogie too.
The frontier's Florence Nightingale.

Custer, she was more than a prostitute,
an *assassine-squaw*

First met up with her long about '75. Business was off so
rooming cottages built and ladies called for to occupy them.

They was of the sporting variety, would have to be wanna come to Fort Laramie. Common like Jane. Her and some few others followed General Crook and when General Merritt sent wagons back home the women rode with the wounded.

Tongue River

      The gold rush was a period in American
      history when men were digging and mining.

          Oremos, oremos
          angelitos somos,
          del cielo venemos
          a pidir oremos

of riches and respect, out of gulches
came jealousy, destruction of the unseen.

          ...we little angels
          from heaven come
          to ask for treats

      selves, hearts, and emptiness

Spectral
War vets sit
Armless

Encrusted black
Marble
Plowshare

Hero infatuations
And Methodist
Prohibitions

Painted sex
Front-tier stage
Ghosting tips

Chartreuse plumes chanteuse.
Cheyenne. *Le chuk wagon.*
Young muscled whackers,
Triple-barreled and stallion-tailed

Deadwood, New Dakota
Derring-do boom
Gold Black Hills

From Kingdom Come
Calam & Wild Bill
Parade down Main

Donned in buckskin, in beaver,
hammered silver, the sun
children, five men

And Jane joins the pageantry
on horse, not prospector
but sentimentalist scout

The Queen with rosemary
potpourri and cowhands
never bedded sober
or pennies in her pocket

                to awaken on a familiar cot and recall a fairy tale

"You're a wonderful little woman to have around in times of calamity,"
says Captain Egan, when I save his life.

                To awaken in an unfamiliar fairy tale

Letters to yourself,
inflammation of bowels
weaver and vowel lover

sense of restriction, like touch

part of her
life nutrient

confessions encoded
in the photo-album
diary of a surface
wound

Your rest in her sleep

Master says, "With your eyes, what have you
Seen? With ears, what have you heard?
What have you said with your mouth?

"As none of these was ever practiced

"From where come such colors, sounds, and scents?"

Be not afeard. The isle is full of noises

Hat Creek
Calamity Peak
Drunk at Jack's Bar
Fell in a lake

Relationship with memory,
the dark star

"Deadwood Dick,
Rider of the Lugubrious Hills"
Disaster

(Now, isn't that rich)

Beautiful white devil of the Yellow
Stone, Heroine of Whoop-up,

In the melodramatic role
Calamity Jane she expounds

(Tight as a three-leg goat)

Billings, Montana, *Gazette*.
Daughter of Janie & Wild Will
Exclusive. Mother's secret diary.
Her confessions. Her letters.

The real Calamity Jane for one dime only

Her deeds and miscredits

Student asks, "Are clouds
running from or chasing the moon?"

"With your mind, what have you fathomed?" replies Master.

Basic fears never materialize
Wherever the body travels
Hometown strangers send it back

    of characters she once was

As in the Noh play, when the lover
Arrives at noon to find no reflection
Alive, she collects change of dreams

    after the lust is gone

They can meet in different parts

    previous world

Shadows lengthen
in anticipation of shades

Replace the word *power* with...
The costume of one's sex.
Passion for male clothes
and companionship
a paradox-mask.

"Pard we will meet again
in the Happy Hunting Ground
to part no more," the stone signature,
written, not in letters, but in her
where signatures of all things
can never be erased, ceased
the afterglow

gun

Imaginary

Hog ranch on the outskirts
Institute for Ladies and Gayeties

to accept her
sleep as his access to her pleasure

exhibit her
exclusively
cow-craft

Bill she thinks she is
And discovers the cruelty
of identities, difference

Forces of air into peaceful
movements; sound
(gentle and
directional)
reveals
the deep
vertebral column

They weave sashes and blankets
Swap stories

migrations over imaginations

orchestrated

held in irons for that which they depend upon

one custodian must
bear the water jar

must gather
clay, shape, and fire

beside the power
behind the prayer of ocean

will draw water from the distant
moon without end

until the sky is dry
her eyes

witness
herself

A door above
your head left ajar
for the emergence

of far-off planets
echoing eloquence toward
bottom

They switch the date of death
to coincide with Bill's
and bury her by his side

Which animals befriend her?
the cat, the kite, the mule:
stubborn, hunter, stray

Le Diable Blanc
at the Number 10 Saloon
Mount Moriah

broken light and grasses
chilled in winter glass
a double sunset

That you choose to destroy but save
instead is the purest act of love.

From GHOSTS!

Tribute to H.D.

In Corfu With Freud

I sit in a hotel room, await my father's return. He is with his lover. I, who sit,
Awaiting Freud

Tear jars
       Tense
              Unable to specify the time I mean, the meaning of time

He tells me to stop checking my watch, to trust
My old Janus, guardian of doorways and roads, beloved light-house keeper,
                              Keeper of the journeying sun

With him I anoint my father's anger, my father's tenderness
Sometimes the twins are sisters

A constellation, circumstance to fit
The garden that corresponds to sky:
Vase of cut stars placed at the temple bough

Like transparencies set before candles in a darkened room
Batlike thought-wings / winds
Confined space of a wicker cage   flickering wicks
Adoring souls, wicked
News of war broke in me   He said, *Trust I will not let you break*
He would take me to a world geographically to my dreams
Greece!
Where I saw the writing-on-the-wall   (*Now Gnostic*) Know Thyself

He believed I roamed through dangerous walled cities
Events out of time
What's it like outside ??? he asked.   Chalked swastikas down Berggasse
    Fortunes that divine "Hitler gives bread"
               To greet the return of the Gods
                                 We roam through dangerous times
Dolls of pre-dynastic Egypt
Thought-winds carry me /   Search-light search
     A dim shape forming on the wall. Foaming swells. Finding
Orange trees in full fruit and flowers outside the window.
    Osage-orange. The walls were ochre.
The house in early shadow. Light on shadow not the other way around.
    Object projected from my brain, basin, buried mind
    Washstand / saucepan or tripod
    Of prophecy. Our thoughts translated into
    Secreted language. Entombed.

Monument wall / will

Between ink, space flies, flanked by butterfly and dying

        Psyche

Death: You can't always get more than your due.
Apollo: We weep when the goods are destroyed

And how do we know when he has died   ??? When we walk down Wall Street and see no Centaurs—Centaurs who once felt everything…

[The following scene takes place in a room on the other side of the wall.]

This is said by me and a voice I'm overhearing that would say what I'd say, if I were in the next room on the other side of the wall:

> I am disturbed he has no idea death won't kill him
> He will shed his locust-husk
> The sun-conscious world of sleep—
> That final healing when he sloughs off his skin.

*

If a woman plants herself by a river,
Gods of trees, air, water
Grace her as a poplar, mulberry, laurel

Globes of gold
Apples, flecked with russet
A skeleton leaf

Her daughter bears the weight of the lost
Child—Even after she's agéd, wizened.
Mother folds her up and places her
In the fifth pocket, the daughter and a poem.

        Outlined in shadow—a lone symptom or inspiration

Sappho

Shaft of scarlet lilies, crushed hyacinth, sea-grass gold,
Leaf melody of unfinished rhymes, of rocky rhythms; rocks
Polished by water
                       Water beating ragged edges; they are never finished,
Flowers blow through flowing water, not a streaming song
But water's wayfaring spirit, its crystal myrtle berry.

The daughter of God
Chariot pulled by sparrows aquiver
And none alive remembers you, gray among ghosts

Niké, the winded runner, the wingless runner, the girlish black-eyed girl.

Desire has shivered her skeleton,
Leaf of the osage-orange flutters in charmed air.
From inside out she shakes to escape.
The ache of dancing flame pillages her walls of flesh and downy hair.

Chats To Cats

The Old Man of the Sea, Sigmund Freud, stood before me.
He stands before me now, seventy-two years later.
A little lion-like creature totters in my direction.
Everyone carries an animal in them.

War is not over.

Our deep place where we hate—where Thoth and Apollo reside,
Riding a gap-toothed goat.

Last night Freud heard the familiar siren-shrieks, then the soul-shattering "all clear."

Danger is out there—the Professor's eternal preoccupation, occupation.

Nemean lion clearing birds from the mind's rafters, fate.

Planting his steadfast foot in the stream of consciousness
Each line in a poem can't avoid acting as a series of questions
That stands half-hidden in the river reeds, watching over
A life that's being born. This is life—see!

This is a frail bridge, strong enough for the Gods who weigh little.
His is a bridge only few can cross.
The building construction
Of phantasms across the bridge are lines of poetry. We reach deep
Inside ourselves and become Gods, light enough to pass, to cross
The rickety bridge over to a housing project
Made of poems. —Mid-income.

He is comfortable leaving this set of phenomena

Guardian of all beginnings

Spiritual Mathemathics

Sex ecstasy in the buried garden.
                         Unconscious
Dominion. Birdcrumbs
         Follow flight backward on the screen,
Against all odds, to some original time.

            Unrecognizable now that he's
                       The stuff of cloud—
       As though space could rest. Sound
                               Connecting lies to truth.

If negative integers (-1, 12) constitute pre-quantities—
in this instance pre-birth—; and if positive integers
constitute present quantities, such as a tiger flying
through air; then what manner of integer would describe
this tiger whose flight [escape] ceases while
his force springs forth? The tiger is no longer pre nor qua
but remains matter, neither created nor destroyed.
What ghost sum accompanies his breakaway?

A conjunction of two ideas, impossible to unite without her
              So delicate,
                     Imperceptible but here
       Remains.

With eyes open she echoes that dream. Fabricates a world,
                      Forgets, or awakens
                                        Onto alternate scenes
    Hides in her mother's voice,
                Offbeat talents, mascara,
                                The seditious garden.

        In the empire of stars
            A sun determines
                A body's course.
    She extinguishes a candle, burns incense,
Suns of many colors shine.
    Now aqua, now lavender,
            Divergent waves reflect back
                  A solar system of give-and-take.

Another view. Imagine: negative integers constitute pre-birth;
0—that nothing but space-and-balance
    Circa (?) living;
        And positive integers,
                postlife,
The infinity we're ! to face

Whose likeness from vacuumed mass is loosed on the world?
        Whose feline eyes?
    Here are photographs with webbed illumination
        Pixilated showers,
            Raw exposures, too contrasted to reckon
        Like staring through a star.

She asks over silence,
        Evades contact through stillness, remoteness
           That threatens a flier, obscures
    A species of spirit that leaps into fog,
              Commits suicide of sense.

If she inverts the graph on which her point is plotted,
                                She will vanish
        Unable to see the circle's center,
           To know herselves:
                  The moon's migraine,
                    Uproarious pregnancy.
        O tiger beyond physics.

CRIMES OF LIVING > **THE PERSISTENCE OF PASSION** > WOMEN IN THE WINDOWS

When her pictorial world dissolves into color
      Replicating nature from within
           Its breathing
           Space.
For instance, not perceiving the persistence of light in her life
       Despite intermittent beams / That
       Which is impossible to perceive / hides
In Time.
  Programmed into the brain, it moves her
 From one scene to the next. The way she arrives anyplace is a mystery.

Her ride, relatively flicker-free. Though...

Stills sometimes linger, still

    Sometimes

    She can't believe
    She's moving.

& If she suffers insight into her limited perspective, then what?

If she glimpses dark periods of nothingness that compose half her frames?

Invisible sites define narrative /

Invisible lives /

      *

In the booth, vortex of powers turned on.
                                         Keep 'em in the dark
He shouts while his female projection emotes
Of a near fatal accident.
                    (As though that's not our entire lives.)

The detour he takes through the matter of women,
              Upmappable terrain / cut, bleed, splice, wrap!

        He touches her / _art
        The blind spot
        Buried between arm and wing

Seeing motion
             As psychological illusion. What can be /
                        [Believed]

When her cell dissolves and revolves
           Not in a past but a parallel ever-present
                   More than one Martine simulcast—

A river of film

APPROXIMATION OF MYSELF > **WOOL AND WATER** > MYO'S SECRET DELIVERY

Shadowman sculls a silhouetted ferry,

memento mori, hauling fishes or silver strand,
River of stars; sky of leaping fish,

When Myo received that luminous night,
"Cleansed of sores go home without your body—
Someone will present you to yourself."

Her current switches
Calming, common

She steps into a lemon eclipse—erotic blue

& Resigns moon viewing until late autumn
As senses fell a winter tree & light
In a backyard falls unobstructed, lets
Like blood from a vein.

Clay of waves, waveforms, essential tensions seeking equilibrium

Dream wounds with vast structures of inner life, in her life,
or her brain limits the speed of emotion-thought, assigns meaning.
The chemical reaction responsible for significance
or order of events critical to the development of self-image.

    In a city of edifice, buildings reign
      Musical space-time

Confluence of forces
Intangible

    Parting wings, panting winds, braving deeps

Or electromagnetic force divines the ocean floor toward her,
What she feels when walking east and west. A map made of inflection,

Implication

Still, before this moment *this* moment
Hadn't existed. Time as an organizational device—such as a filing cabinet
No repeating *This*. Proxy.
Approximation [of who I was] (She). The ersatz attempts to stay
Awake, will continue to be her [the old me, the newer one to come]
                            Though by another animator
                                    Imitator.
                                Wander-souls seek suicide.

Who sees the change in gods? I mean guards.

With the notion of erased time, it has been tough for dreamers of late.
                                        Not just eternity but infinity.

"Well, I'll eat it," said Alice / Myo. "And if it makes me grow larger, I will reach the key, and if it makes me grow stronger, I'll creep under the door, so either way I'll get into the garden, which is *all* that matters!"

> Our investigation is grammatical, sheds light on our problem by clearing away misunderstandings between forms of expression in different regions of language.

To be dying is to be living, to be living is to be dying.

If the Hara is empty spirit, as we wander through form. Sound mountain. Wind engenders time. Breath: wind. Nonwind, nonbreath engenders timelessness. Non-lessness. For those who have re-leased breath, housed in it, firing down freeways. Relinquish.
Clinking bell.

This Matter beyond correspondence

So, for instance, love is syntactical in nature, protected by sexual organ.
                                    Certain aspirations nontransferable.

                    The similarities between the sentences, "I'll keep it in mind" and "I'll keep it in this box" can lead one to think of the mind as a thing like a box with contents.

The doctor instructed, "You must not give her any more till your lips are quite rested." "But, you see, Doctor, I owe her a hundred and eighty-two."
Tears ran down the doctor's cheeks, and he offered, "Send your kisses in a box."

The muscles of your mind will tire out if you believe such impossible things, and you'll grow so weak you won't be able to believe the simplest true things.

One hundred eighty-two kisses arrived Special Delivery, I believe.

Inventers of mirrors and minor notes. Venters of anger. Venders of illusion.
The illusion that time is an excuse to forget only *this* instant exists.

Though she has identity plates to drive through a lucid state, the order of critical events altered and she has became other

That things might change or cease, that they might not

And so it was: she, now, only ten-inches high, and her face brightened at the thought that she was the right size for going through the little door into that lovely garden.

In the garden of melody, listen to shiny stones, harp sparrow, and the wavering road. Weeds overtake plot. She roots them out, the din, colors, cloud evanescent

If nothing is true than anything is possible.
    We are creatures in minds
        Of others: musk, lichen,
            Bits of landscape, stamen
  Assorted forms simultaneously

To remember *love* has no one
                                Meaning.

Desire opiating the present. Before she knows it
A variety of bodies have been lived in
[Nightshade, touch-me-not],
One minded like the weather, most unquietly.
Collected miracle, collective miracle.

APPROXIMAYION OF MYSELF > WOOL AND WATER > **MYO'S SECRET DELIVERY**

Myo said speech defines water levels. Saliva, pond, proud body;
Aquavit ocean and disrobing it. Robbing its moods, moaning waves,
Deepening roots,
      Intensely intellectual and erotic, expands form, mind ground
           How a fluid transports her surrender,
                            beneath her
Lips and tongue stir mindlessly
Breath cruises the unexplored
When someone enters your life and jolts you into fluency.

She was sent an attachment, only 30KB; couldn't open the file or
Leave [love, believe] herself.

    (he, the attachment she tried to detach from. Contained movement
                                    Of a present
        Dreamroom, abound WorldWideWeb.com
        Not minding no-mind or that knot
            Apart from her,
                Not part of her)

    Self-secrets uncovered in mediary diaries with once-removed memory
                            Scribed as being-time

    A soul-stone the size of Polaris
        Stored in a mason jar & crammed with lost buttons from bygone eras
            Or stuffed with nuts and bolts,
                Simple / greasy

Miles of her. Separate.

Indigenous deities, mountain sprites.

Myo lives TiVo

      Computer headspace, digitalized storage,

How she organizes herself / time internally. Mental tempura.
                                    In- and outside travel
Varying speeds, multitudinous directions.
            Ouch!

Monk A: What have you done in a lifetime?
Monk B: Eaten a little midday and slept a few hours at night.
Monk A: Tilled the land, harvested its cornucopia. Shared it.
    Sun falls through the belly of mountain. Moon
    Pocks earth with shadow. Oceans wave &
    Boulders crumble. Nothing
                                  Special.

The wizard speechifies: One is judged not by how deeply one loves
but by how deeply one is loved—[couldn't be further from the truth]
    We seek it far away, what a pity!

Invisible thread or Borg-like interdependence
                While reckless gods build firewalls

The metaphysics of self-conception
                Paves a perpetual identity destiny (the etiology
                      Between attachment to self and independence
                              {In-dependence
                              Deep-time comprehended
In a trance
        Vanished.

Like Osiris who was gathered from land- to bodyscape
I re-member my father by my heart
Sow him from pieces of me (father from my truth)
The wondrous phenomenal mansion of who I became
Without thinking

The vase body

Flickering of a lantern like the light of firefly, friendly fire, like prana roused
Out of Code Blue
My self-vision bleeding to emptiness
Wires, pipes, tubing or
Puffins loosed with red ribbons dangling off wings,
Beautiful but still
Strings, so attached to freedom, to sky
Mind capturing
Mirror of insight, walking through the town of appearances,
Apparitions of intelligence, edifice, elevator.

Based on hearing
The awareness-holders
Protected over lifetimes
By the heart practice.
Secret Master Hero Stainless Steel—subway, take me,
After which I'm dissolved. As a result, realizations spontaneously spring.
Vital Wind blows. I forget about the appearance of life. My father was heroic,
Nonmaterial, nonactual.
My code breaker. Not making it known, even to the wind-ear transmission.
We gather with inner offerings. Offing.
Impermanency rings in the concept of notions. Suture-needles & needs & pins
Undermine metaphysics of the individual (underpinnings), rendered empty
Because of the proximity of death—who I am without you.

Living with Animals

    Her room lit by the cache of a thousand creatures
                                   Their thorny hooded habits

She catches her keep.
With shrew-nets, dream-rods.

                              *

    Nocturnal spirits play secretive, rarely seen,
                      Most at home on ground
                                Though happy to climb trees

Or hyphenate wing and air—soaring through the transparent prison,
        Partaking in oral transportation,
        Moving through sound and speech.

                              *

None lightened without adding lightness
    Flavor for euphony
Like cheesecake batter in a yellowware bowl.

        Craft the body spiritual and it will glow,
        A moon spoon for mixing words,
How co-life aspires.
Headlamps hold night-frogs. Dixie Cups, polliwogs.

*

In falling from the sky and floating, a melody
    Leaves
        Its unfinished line
            In memory

            The soul's sphericity. Through marbleized
            Eyes. Tambourines.
                Cat's harlequin carnival.

*

A round-up of abstracted Arabians
Hazy paint drays
    Quicken / drear
    Variation of song and sense.
    In one fugue state or another
    This fairy ring of yearlings trailing an areola along
                          Insect's iridescent wing.

*

    Aristophanes, Hitchcock
        Draw light on imaginings
            Hawk & owl descend during new moon
    Unlike cumulus cloud pets, the dispossessed
X-ray through darkness
        Break an oath that binds bird to bird.

A constellation of warblers undulate in sealed captivity. By her bedside
        Rests a jar of black glass
            She breathes the breath of flight
Cardinal points.

*

Once upon a time, they shed
        Their scales,
                Tumbling into undifferentiated reverie.

Pressure on night's reduced darkness
                Or failure to adhere
        To demands of the waking dead: Their double, amphibious lives
        Perpetually encircling a soul on the verge of escape:
                              The haunt.

Cubist Winds

To discover a tree in his ear,
Birds in that tree.
A clearing, charmed stream
Coils the breeze.

                    Sibilance
                    Sibilance

Everything's motile
Composed of iron (for might),
                Sulfur (change),
                            Water (flexibility)
Add dust and dearth.

                    *

When hurricane emanates a void
        The impermanence of beauty

        Doors swing inward
                An opening onto himself.

                    *

    If one walks through a front
    Visibility gloom;
        Instilled with the immeasurable dimensions
    Of spirit, though blind to his nature—a weatherscape in proportion
        To what she trusts is
                Not pure emptiness.

The way an easterly
        Penetrates him
Cave-swallows
        Excavate,
Tunnel through his know-how or nest
In naturally occurring holes. How he struggles to receive deities
        Sacred bondage

        Whisper song
             Between wind & weather

      *

        An intellectual   *mistral*
        Passionate   *sirocco*

        Frightened   *willy willy*
                           Lightning
                                   Up its elephantine trunk
                                   Out through branches and leaves
                                   If roots are damaged, its line dies

                Cloud lore
                Passerine

            With an eyedropper
            Kidnapping delicate dreams
            Progeny of intimacy.

                        *

Identifying the course his mind rages,
Its incline and turbulence.
                The *haboob* spiraling sand thousands of feet above.
                            Specks disseminating
                     Light-years westward
                          Dust chokes memory
                                Clogs the heart.

How to find land when winds have left atmosphere structurally damaged

    The loss of his glow system. Pool
Filled with sunbeams. Currents float hollow stalk and bone.

        Even a container (exists / doesn't) for winds
        Ocean basin, brain,
                Crusty earth storing magma
Luminous little begging bowl of vibrant determination.

        *

    If small clouds of late noon melt on dusk,
    The gentleness of dawn
            Dew, frost,
            Fog evaporate
            As though they never were.

That which appears
As opposed to what is. Optics or perspective.

    Answers run out
               Like breath
                  How a cone connects cloud with
        Surface
            Of water-whirling air
An inland phenomena that occurs when radiance first
                Reflects on his face.

Dearest,

In the summer of 365, when the sea withdrew in Cyprus
And stone was spewed from the living earth, young parents
Cradled their offspring in burning flesh and tenderness.
The father, arching like a pediment, sheltered his wife
From entombing mortar. His arms shielding her
Breasts. The supple flesh of their four hands
Protecting baby's skull and spine. Snapped neck, wing
Bone clipped. How heroic and fragile
They are, stilled for eternity before dawn.

This morning, the sun streaks magenta and tangerine.
A deep calm stifles the earth.
When you withdrew, stone and fire were hurled into the heavens,
Torn asunder. So fragile are tendon, synapse, which plait
And protect love. The hard parts that fossilize, soft parts
Vaporize, like shadow-remnants of a nuclear storm. Buried
Memories quake. My love, what is left
This daybreak as we rise in the quiet and safety of our shelters?

As ever,

Finding my way back from the underworld.

From WABAC Machine

Cat

The cat belongs to
Me. The cat belongs
To the house. The cat belongs to
The other cat. The cat
Belongs to itself. The cat
Belongs to the forest. The
Cat belongs to the bird and mouse.
The cat belongs to the mountain lion.
The cat belongs to no one. The cat
Belongs to nothing. The cat belongs
To everyone, everything.

The cat has a name
That I gave it. Everyone knows the cat's name
Is not its name. It is *my* name for the cat.
Sometimes the cat refuses to acknowledge
This name and sometimes the cat
Plays along with the life I've created for the cat.
Sometimes the cat pretends that it doesn't live in a realm
Different from the one that the cat and I
Live in together. The cat has needs that must be met
For the cat to live in my house, though most of the cat's time
Is spent elsewhere. I invite the cat to live with me
So I can perceive some of the "elsewhere"
In which the cat spends much cat time.
The cat shares what I can't see by maintaining
An existence in my house and by responding to
The name I gave the cat.

I know there will be a moment
In the circuitry of space-time in which the cat will discard
The name and forsake my house for good
And will exist only in the fields
I cannot see without the cat living in my house. On that day,
I might say, "The cat has moved full time into the wild."
Or I might say, "Miau-miau has run away."

Customers Who Bought "Sleeping Beauty" Have Also Bought This

ME. Pron. The objective case of I.
1. *A state in New England.*
2. *ME, a concept in the cosmology of Sumerian mythology.*
3. *Net energy available in certain foods.*
4. *A think group that resides in my head. A large, furry animal. A Me. The me.*
5. *A bullet's point of entry.*

Upon awakening from a story, before walking through the portal to the hallway into a land where language is required, I confirm I'm ME (a state in New England) (a think group). Some days I don't arrive at the threshold of my body and a deep, cavernous loss resides where ME would have been. The cave paintings in Lascaux. Horses, bulls, and stags—motifs that repeat when I can't see where I'm headed, when I'm in a forest. Some days I ingest donuts and sour dough, some days I sleep deep in mud, like a fish that wants to stop drifting, day into night into day.

I stand before the portal / window / screen door (or other port of entry). Beside ME (a large, furry animal) appears another ME (of Sumerian mythology). Look, I have spread! Mother feels my finger and knows that it has grown.

A little girl with 100-year-old crone legs wakes from her blackout.
She hands a poison apple to a drop-dead beauty. One must wonder
What she's hiding under her dress. In her heart. The apple spiked with E.

"Mirror, mirror inside ME
        Spinning out fate
                Who do WE hate?"

The beauty bites. SLEEPS *(sleep meaning a cheap way of travel, a calming narcotic, a monk with mu mind—verb, passive and active)*.

She rushes through an hour like a hallway. The alarm rings as she attempts to outrun the wolf, the wind. Music imprisoned by its bars (the breath of bars and their throbbing beer-soaked walls). Flesh and time swap outfits—either way, a jailor enforces a life sentence. Either way we wither.

I eye her through a mirror. She eyes me as I sleep through life—
> lying / dreaming that I'm a fairy princess,
>> A God-fearing goblin A talking bird.

<u>I am none of these</u>.
> *not this knee, not this shyness, not this halo…*

I take the shortcut through the forest. I ax down trees. I chop off hair. I revise the story. I win. I live; still, I am eternally forever after.

Smoothing out despair
Isn't as easy as steaming wrinkles from silk to be worn by Cinderella.
She took the remedy out of an old story
By painting herself into a dream
Of self. Mostly air disturbs
The sea // mostly light (noon light), parabolic light,
Finding the tree distinct from its color. Poison knowledge.
On the threshold of land where language is required. I dream
I am hiking among weinheimers that scamper through pet doors
Into a past and recite "Howl." We clap paws and run sharp claws
Across a pearlescent moon. Morning fog unwraps pond
To reveal a soggy sandwich. The wax paper is oily, transparent—
Through it I see diverse divinities running
The Greatest Show on Earth, now playing
On a distant planet called Barnum & Bailey—
Its deities: misfits, freaks, manifestations of me.
In order to talk to her, I have to enter her world
And remember precisely who she is / I am.
Once there, I arrive at Mother's
Who is cavernous, a dark space painted with primitive stags, bulls, horses.

Hard Objects Found in People

Jailbirds in striped jumpsuits that can't be seen through bars
                Angry prisoners known to drag around balls and cat bells

         Hungry ghost prisoners
         Turrets occupied by armed prison guards
                Smoking hot terrine with four and twenty blackbirds

      [breath of bird]
The curve of his chest
Pressing against blades of grass to carve the nest

When a dreamer considers tenderness
               Wears his demeanor like a bullet-proof vest,
Considers psychoanalysis
When a dreamer dreams a wren considering a nest egg, annuities

     When the dreamer and wren dream of transporting the telepathic girl /

Saint Anthony, patron saint of lost items (girls, birds, prisoners)
Saint Adrian, of butchers, of arms dealers and prison guards

When Saint Anthony and Saint Adrian met at a
confession convention at Santa Barbara, they
were magnetically pulled into each other's
booths and naturally chose one another when
it came time to reveal their hearts.

                Space of a camera Time of a camera

The *vaulted chamber* of prison extended to our chats
       In our hearts, more Gothic chambers
         Ghost chambers…

    A canopied forest protected
    His mind from high winds
    If he weren't dreaming he'd be flying

Even love requires immigration officers. Expiration
Dates. Identification after death. I'm surprised
At how completely we can disappear.
I'm surprised at how we can't *completely* disappear
Even though we were insignificant when alive.
Even though we spent our lives in prison.

Even love requires irrigation, irritations

The telepathic girl—a transparent configuration
     Though with no parent
    Unconscious data, too
    Withdrawn

No sewing notion

The cat broke out of prison,
    Bonelessly slipped into *invisible times*. Disquietly appeared

Why set up surveillance cameras? Those presence chambers that catch
  Clips of meaningless winged felines chasing contrail birds
  Building nests in the eaves of prisons—parallel lives that fade
  From focus to focus. Liquid dreams of cats.
      Tell me who haunts you

Time doesn't move (has no hands, no legs, surely no heart)
                But is the median out of which we float

(Sewing time / knowing)

Halls encircled by trees
Hells
Rêves

                The Gratitude holiday parade included a giant Dora the Explorer helium balloon and a prison float. The inmates, dressed in jumpsuits, catcalled our guards and executioners.

Cameras flashed. Smiles.

"Happy Gratitude" was hollered at the top of their lungs as inmates jumped in unison

Birds in V formation hovered above veiled revolutionaries dressed as saints

The city's dream face, its stronghold and revolving doors

The Mountain

山是山
mountains are mountains

Small waterfalls girdle the rural hotel. To its left, a sinuous stream sinks razor-rock teeth into the earth. During rainy season, the surround-sound can be deafening, but in the dead of winter, when the stream and falls freeze over, form hovering petrified cliffs of ice—eyeteeth of ice transmogrified *and even the birds have flown south, nothing, nothing*, even the air hibernates—the hotel, which is my new home, is the quietest spot anywhere. At night, during the wolf moon, the hotel's guests arrive: the celebrated actress, the skiing champion, and the CEO of a Fortune 500 company. They cross a rickety wooden bridge and are bundled in woolen mufflers and rugged mountain boots, wear hand-stitched undies sewn out of coarse fabrics. They've discarded their treasures, reminders to themselves and the world of what they've achieved, of their aches, their bruises and burdens, their black holes—diamonds, medals, fine fountain pens—and they march onward, pressing against the contours of the craggy mountain, blinded by crystallized white. When they arrive at the hotel, they leave behind their charisma, expertise, their ability to make their way in the world. The hotel is in the mountain's shadow, safely tucked away from harm. During their stay, they forfeit that which resides in their pasts. During their stay, moonlight can be seen reflected in a dewdrop, and the light of a dewdrop can be seen in the moon

When I'm not at the hotel, I'm perpetually preparing speeches for the Oscars; I'm the one who's replaced Lindsey Vonn in Vancouver; the indispensable decision-maker who oversees captains of industry, my unmitigated lust for achievements, a voracious hunger for triumph and illimitable accolades. I wander urban streets on the prowl for love. Gaping. But when I'm in the hotel

The sleeping parts, streaming arts…I leave dreams at the door with my shadows, my shoes, no footprint…I leave open the door

*

The day she first found the hotel was most unremarkable. She was lost (the hotel wasn't), looking for a gas station in what appeared to be deserted, mountainous country; what she'd describe as *empty*. Her tank, too, was near empty, and she saw a roomy house with a sign that read "vacancy," a rooming house that appeared vacant. She had mentioned before coming upon the hotel that she had wanted to break into the central story of her life, that she lived on the stage set of a fictional small town, and it was time to pack up and move out

Curiously, the rural hotel had a revolving front door so the boundary between inside and out was undefinable. Curiously, the rural hotel was furnished with escalators, conveyor belts, moving walls, Murphy beds, so where one was one moment varied in the next, varied in the text, so when she read about herself she became, and when she fell asleep—book in hand—she was over

When winter turns to night. When night winterizes, turns to light. What she didn't know was that something entered her dreams from time to time and disconnected her, and returned her to her present life with pieces missing, words lost, broken or forgotten parts, fragments, and at other times this someone stole from others places utopian or dystopian landscapes, "self-scapes," to place inside her. What she didn't know was that sometimes what she hated in the world had been taken from *her* gallery and hung on others for her to view without the obstruction of self distorting her perceptions or reactions, an amusing diversion for one who took pleasure in toying with sentient beings. She didn't know one moment from the next, though she pretended to. Time to move out, move on, to stop pretending

Sometimes a slow storm would roll over her, as happens on prairies during prayer

Sometimes she'd wake from a snowy blackout

The blackout was around her head, then her heart, from interior to exterior, living room to breathing room

She saw it or dreamed it or was it

During a storm she watched it through a window

They studied it in school

The factory that she worked in produced it
Procured it

Her cheek pressed against frosted glass, a cold chuck of her heart

Sometimes a slow storm would roll over her or through her or she, herself, was the storm

She'd weep

She'd blow out an inconceivable amount of wind

She'd pretend to sleep   to pray

She'd pretend not to be dying   not to be killing   she'd pretend to be seeing (not to be stealing, not to be lying, not to be defiling) what was before her what she was before

The doctor studied her corpse as well as the corpses of others. She couldn't quite feel him probing, more along the lines of she "sensed" him carefully studying her spinal column, the architecture of her neck. She wondered what made her different from others or the same, or why he studied her structure when air had been frozen out of her for such a long, long time. The halting of sound, wind blowing against the mountain, eroding rock. Dust. Ash. *How long has winter been upon us?* she wondered. The bridge swaying. Pilgrims rocking with the bridge. She's on her way to the hotel. She's right behind him. In the lab, the doctor rests his hand on the small of his back, scratches his temple

She's under…through…in   wind…snow   pressed against…placed over to be killing…to be dying…to be passing…turning…the mountain's spine… craggy column   its breath…its life…its death

She passed over the mountain. She walked through gusts of snow. Praying. Turning from winter into spring, from the dead of night into pre-dawn. Into light

He closed his eyes. His loved ones surround him. A mountain on all sides. Always. In all ways. *What's behind the lid?*

for Keith Sheaffer

The Gossamer Tincture

She poured herself a glass of yellow—treacly yellow trickling down her throat, tricky yellow, causing her to lose steam, yellow light streaming from the sun and bleaching daisies yellow:

> yellow jackets snuggled into their yellow jackets for the winter deep in jaundiced earth, awakening to a shovel's nudge as she plants her daffodils, and with little warning, the earth warming, yellow jackets swarm about her, a golden diadem of doom.

As a young bride, her husband would shower her with small tokens of affection—scarves, earrings, kittens. Each day she'd traverse the wrought iron spider bridge at the end of her lane that spread in six directions. Her scarf would fly from her neck and drift on the breeze, an earring would unhook and disappear in the dark water below spider bridge, a kitty would squirm out of her basket, and its siblings would stretch to fill the momentary space it left behind. She believed she might break the spell that bound her to loss.

It is an illusion, we all now know, one of the greatest in fairytales, as well as one of the greatest threats—loss of home, of food, of parents. Loss of love. Loss of power.

She poured herself a glass.

Did I mention she had died as a young bride? Though time had not caught up with her, and her death, like her age, did not yet show.

The husband would leave their home in the mornings in a huff and, rather than blow the house down, he would sail out into the wide sea that was his life. And the young bride would putter around the neighborhood, careful not to cross too many legs of spider bridge and get lost with the scarves, her earrings, her little kitties. She lost her way, way too easily. She'd lose her husband's trifles, yes, but more worrisome, she was in danger of losing her name, her identity. And then what? What would become of the young bride who was no longer young? No longer a bride? Already she was no longer alive—that was the one certainty of this tale.

She used to be the sister and wandered directionless in the broad forest with her lost brother. If she hadn't had her wits, she'd be witch fodder like that twin.

She knew her husband lived a secret life separate from his meanderings in the small, thatched cottage they shared together. In a dream, she combed through his pockets and found a map of his daily travels. There on the east side of the map, near where the sun rose, was their life together, while up above and to the west were multitudinous kingdoms, rich with tapestries of eels and unicorns, a firstborn, mint gardens, mind gardens, and fair maidens haunting deep wells, showered, as she was, with small trinkets and favors and magical words. Jealousy is yellow. Drinking calms it.

She poured herself into the glass.

Many cracks defaced her vista:
There was the earth with its small fissures,
The sky with light-chips cracking through,
And the mirror that exaggerated the cracks around her eyes.
There was the fractured ocean, crashing and cracking at the seams with tornadoes
Of light and also a heaviness she could not name.

She was once a young bride

The wedding was joyful, guests elegantly dressed, each bestowing a blessing—some sent songs, others cream confections, and books of poetry with ambrosial words that melted on the young bride's tongue.

Her brother appeared from a shadow. He was moldy, stained, ancient. Though, of course, she knew him immediately. Of course, she loved him still. She'd follow him anywhere. Through the mossy rainforest. Through a dream of a hungry witch. Into an oven, hot and inescapable. Her brother whispered the secret in her ear. The language of the secret is magical. The sound is haunted. Of course, she understood. Of course, she remembered.

We remember, yes. The maps of underground kingdoms, the trifles, the words that lit us up. We remember for a long, long while. And then the meanings transform as simply as characters in fairytales; and "happily" and "ever after" no longer refer to the promise of a perfect future but to a whisper that a long-lost twin poured deep in an ear—a thick, hot yellow whisper, viscous as glass, sticky as treacle, sharp as a stinger, a gossamer whisper we spent our lives trying to lose, a whisper planted in us—and then we break open with dawn, with the sun's treasury, and then we break free

for Malinda Markham

Assemblage

I

They cut up her life into discontinuous stills, a collage of references
With unspecified status—labels on feminine products, mandala diadems

She knitted a sweater of origin. Memory baby planets.

Though if she stopped producing new product,
Reverted to reflection. Mirror of movement /

They placed her in a sphere that acted on her senses, and though her moments
Seemed to adjust to contingencies, the nature of moment
Remained unaltered—a play cast with an unsustained "I": rotating light
That allows the designer to place obstructions on the path so light offers
Alternative routes out of design

How to be a bird, to resize perspective. Dragon power,
Dinosaur power, taking wing to stars,
Forest of ginkgo ocean

She is in the ocean forest, mile-high waves shade the liquid course. She is in
The forest, distant winds susurrating silvery leaf

She is nearing the dream, though it is still
A long way off

II

What happened when all mirrors
Went out, when the gods no longer controlled us

But only our belongings. Who, then, did we belong to? We needed things
To get from here to there. After all, our body, like the breeze,
Passes through us, passes
On. After all, the weather wears us,
After all, our body is contingent

Moist surface of breathing passages
Intercostal muscles
Overwhelming air hunger

How far she traveled through evaporation. Blades of brief belief,
Blue corolla

And it rains into the night,
(Stills of light)
For as far as the eye can imagine.

When they cut up her life into discontinuous stills, it forced her to acknowledge
The momentary, even in octopus sleep, even in starlit dream,
An even blanketing

III

Spider spinning threads
Of pale gold
Drawing the eye drapery
The dewy web that canopies perspective

Something must happen, she told the spider:
The players digress—their lines, webs

Living among so much dead stuff

And the dead, too, must be tended, she was told by the fly

IV

She tries not to hear the tickled stream
Which laughs the mountain, which is the redwoods, which is the slug,
Which is the exhale, loudly leaving the mouth of the mountain
Controlled by the stream's fracture,
The stream that trickles through the mountain

And into the robin, also the mountain, tooting.
Food for forms and worms, yes, all mountain

What's on the other side of the mountain sleeps.

V

The text says, a moving-picture universe displays delusion of connectivity

But stills are still not unified, the telling part
Of a story
Lodged between fact

While, each moment is a connected dot
Launching into air
Mocking
The feathered world below

VI

Nightjar sneezes five
Perfect songs
Unimpaired by the chipped moon

No one is not
Shadows cast under moon's glow.
Even though she is broken, she is able to flow, reflect, immersed
In moonlight, approaching the dream by klieg or follow spot,
On a stream of light brought into question

Chipped moon tooth

Following adventures reverse in time to find the story, the chip

Victims chained to sleep as they attempt
To claw their way back, trapped in a limitless moment,
No different than any other.

The Philosophy of House-Keeping

"She died at play / Gambolled away / Her lease"

*Five Chinese brothers live with retarded cats, wander the edge of the woods in wait. The five brothers with one name, one nature, with five gills, five gifts, housed in one body with five doors. As Emily dreams, she floats to the top floor, head in clouds, laughing helium. A cup of cinnamon tea. She visits the five chiming brothers who save her from drowning, burning, fading, shrinking—nightly she retreats into a spectral episode and the brothers draw her near—sing to her / recite her favorite lies, bouquets of jasmine and buttercup pregnant with songbird scent. A goldfinch Eucharist flutters against her teeth (ooh!), attempts to escape belief. In one dream she's a porn star—wraps her diminutive thighs around a pole, how she wraps her mind around death, poem after pole, after poem, and then she's dressed in Frankenstein's creation—her bodice and crushed girdle, a patchwork of putridity. Baking loaves of gingerbread**, sifting sugar, licking tears from hummingbird eyes, always she's Emily recalling a world in a house, objects in a kitchen—desire, hope, love—now*** rolling pins, an herbarium, the wire mousetrap. She embraces each noun that will vanish when she dies to the nothing it came from—the word—the way a cloud pie**** flies like a bee buzzing past the ear, flakes, and tenderly melts. Night blows out the single star for fear.*****
Trombone air. Troubadour.

Notes:
*A poem without "I" wanders purgatory, swims through tormented seas of unsewn sheaves, travels farther into summer than birds.
**The lost chapter on bread baking.
***Language is a machine that brings abstractions into being, semiconductor that permits contact between light wave and light bulb; its antonym, "death," acts as a microtransformer of objects, reversing them into concepts. Without the authority of one fatal tongue, words fall into the vast vat of sound.

****Place ½ cup of cloud in glass bowl. Saturate with lemon water. A pinch of salt from teardrops. Introduce feathery chartreuse, magenta, cobalt, and cream—slowly fold in memories of pleasure until light and well blended.
*****Without a child she will always be a broken pine, burning in the oven.

Commentary:

She who wrote: "To die—takes just a little while—/ They say it doesn't hurt"
As a specialist in dying and a meticulous record-keeper
Of the dead, she inhabited a world that could be trusted
To forget.

The Secret Conversing of Birds

Sometimes it starts with a murder of crows congregating on an echoing field
Of Persian onions in bloom, wild leeks, crimson poppy.
Caw, caw, the crow circles its cry, never returning
To the taking-place, the spin-off point, as if Doctor Maximus, of theosophical
Speculation, donned in body's negative dervish-frock, swims
The earth's solid breath (*ku? ku? where? where?*). Is he listening to melodic
Hammering at the goldsmith's smithy? Dancing for hours, never
Turning twice, as if the good doctor were exiled in the flesh
Of Rumi where illuminations join at an interior and anterior edge, where everything
Is the same, only somehow something is not—his feminine tears
Submerge the bolted landscape as they mutually dissolve. With loss
Of motion goes memory, with collapsed space our dervish halts,
Utterly alone, uttering to strings of light—*ku? ku?* he says—*ku ku,* they reply
Into his shelter of thought that forms a hapless desire for
A deep divine homelessness, as if homelessing amounts to attaining or being
Initiated into the inspirited spiritualis, as if buildings abruptly refuse
To conceal their exhausting dance, as if we follow our homes
Throughout our lives, as if our lives
Depend on our seeking or seeing
Scrying tears where poeming commences.
As if the ancient dances of homing and whirling were distinct.
(As we circle our cries to call ourselves home)

Rumi knows the kitchen and weaving places, hemstitching
Fraying seams after the tangerine moon
Has risen, the indivisible sun sets
Behind grenadine syrup—willful, reviled,
There are great mirrors around him,
Bolts of blinding shine reveal
Sunlight swords (sun's words),
Dawn whispers, "Are they coming or going?"
The purple light of reason. What is Great Purple? A season passing.

Dancing above amethyst sand, camels carry souls across the desert—transporting
You and me to our next bodies.
                              I'm a language cashier at a pet shop
Where more dialects are spoken than words in the mega-dictionary.
We carry birds—young parrots with green plumage, a rooster
Who heralds in the Morning Prayer that each species
Diligently attends, as they tend to do. We have <u>the</u> dog of the seven sleepers who sits
Vigilantly protecting their dreams, awaiting their awakening
When they'll feed him the sweet kernel, which contains our most precious oil.
He'll taste the world in it.

I sell temporary kitties in the form of reconstituted sponges.
Place one in a tank of water filled with fresh thoughts
And she'll implode into nuclear color. Down a sliding pond. Licking
Her paws and the eyes of her kitty-cat pals, preening toes and assholes,
Batting around more reconstituted sponges (other temporary kitties).

During winter, peach-faced lovebirds disappear
In the mirror game. They can play forever without striking
Their reflection—the winged body, our technology body
That utters the absolute, resolute, like a figure
Which is uttered into existence.
Water does not issue (rush) out the mouth of a stone bird
But what isn't animated? Even grief, even sleep.
A mountain of skulls.
What isn't animal!

Doctor Magnanimous spinning counterclockwise in a black dervish coat,
His tombstone headdress a reminder that an essential remainder
Coats the earth with who we've been before.
Flying the sky, cackling, careening, dragon bones melting, leopard
Spots fading feathers floating
                    Into snow crystals / icicles / starlight stalactites / faithful dog
Finally fed his desserts justly—ebullient, turbulent, sighing winds shifting and
Turning into whirling birds.

SNOWING OVEN

> *There is nothing but snow*
> *In that white-hot stove.*
> —Jean Arp

When you open your smiling oven, steaming noodles and goodies

*

Some snow leopards sleep on the mount of my tongue—
So adept in hiding are they
That I barely know when they're there

Though sometimes a purr
Melting through me
Pre-heat

*

Open wide—There is nothing in your mouth
Just a wintry mix, groomed trails, slopes—more snowsqualls,
More drifts—I get it, you wouldn't say what was in the oven,
Your mouth closed for the weather,
For winter,
Snow spices
Piquance.
After all, melting is not the same as disappearing.
Your open smile,
Heat

*

If I drill through your snow to the hidden lake region
Baking ancient snow, swirling frosting, icing

*

It's snowing; nothing to do but bake!
Always so tempting to open a warm
Fresh smile.

On Becoming a Poem

Three winter wrens
Flute through blinding field—
Their feathered extremities jacketing
Hollow bone, a hole, dear one

Spineless fascicles of ephemera

I've known some birds that appear
As accountants of lost objects. They
Call numbers through karmic arteries,
Scope and tally earrings, scarves, thoughts,
Set telegraphically, telepathically in a holograph storehouse
Deep in inviolate woods.

Percussive memories, plumes drum

Three librarians flutter
Above land neck, land waist
Lore of scythelike wing

Toward gnat's horizon

The philanthropist donates his phantom to a museum
Philomena swallows, weaves
Trace filaments

Faith trails

Swift's song of long glistening notes
At noon, never to be
Seen.* Herself a part of a high March sky

The summer day and bird-call.

*From Emily Dickinson's obituary in the *Springfield Republican*,
May 18, 1886, written by Dickinson's sister-in-law.

The Composer

                    To arrive anywhere intact
          The composer must penetrate the forest. With his imaginaries,
              His aura, aurally
                                The composer translates human praxis
                      Into vernacular knowledge,
    Must pierce body and forest / Fatty earth and the thick bones of trees.

                            *

The composer's imaginaries secrete space & spatial
            Underpinnings that support smaller and smaller forests,
            Microscopic forests, invisible forests
                    (How do you tell the tale of a forest in absent land?)
            Teeny ones full of ghosts and cold
            Female composers low to the ground
            Playing in color / with phantoms / bright dyes
            & bright eyes—waterfalls offering water
            To thirsty spirits
                        Protean forests

            Super-sized ones, spectacular spectacles
            Of colossal filigreed forests

                            *

Beware of criminal ghosts under house arrest in giant trees or housed
In the bodies of animals. A tree kangaroo might know too well
The forest's acoustics, an ancient specter dressed in marsupial skin
Hearing calls the composer will write in the future

            To expand the experience of time
            To display an interior core

                            *

        Even if song were a vehicle driven by frog and monkey,
                        Liberated from the dark / moist
            Forest by the composer writing it into being,

Even if he were born with a dictionary and primer specific to his clan,
Even if he were born with an instruction manual,
                      instructor's guide [answers],
                              cliff
                                  notes,

Even then,
    The exegesis of the composer and his composition would pass beyond sense
                      Ineffable,
              Evanescent,
                      even part mineral. even part criminal.
      The spirit is indeterminate—random neurons—
                Loose wires and red ribbons, unbridled
          [upbraided].
The flexible spirit escapes house arrest,
          Travels wormholes through light-years,
                  Pierces fatty earth and thickened bones of trees,
      Surfaces as the spirit of the forest, the flesh of the forest,
      The composer of the forest.

Spirited Away

        She's a god of birds
        And gods of birds love to bathe
                In Earth's minerals
                              Azure, topaz, graphite, mind

She's a god of birds
        Unbeknownst to her,
                Who works in the bathhouse,

        Bathes boys:
        Frogs

    The god of birds
Oversees boiling moods / traveling soot
                Concocts medicines

To cure memory
As it ages

    During bedtime, she cries in the fountain & it retreats
                                        Abandons

        The god of birds
                Becomes more / or less / of her
                              Disparity

A parrot

Gods of fish fly. Birds bathe.

        A god of birds is what we least want.
        She carries her former self
        In a feathered body bag
        Like a murderer
        Hiding hollow hellos.

    Life in a body is subject to time
                      At all times a subject

                              In a body of weather;

      Spill some in bath water
      And self merges into something other,
                                  Mirage.

As one with wings
                She cannot stay
                The building might take leave at any moment
    Not only its motion but emotion,

Doors and thoughts through tangled hair,
Heart: cupola flooded by drafty light
Flies into rafters. A cooing echo.

The Moving Castle

Music: Koto and shakahachi.
Samurai warriors blow into bamboo weapons, wander identity, passing secrets
Compass: Nexus
        Solaris
           Wonton

Goldfish turn to flame
Swim updraft &
Always Moonbird feathers ▼ , an enchanting veil,
                      Mini-verse stitched in a bonnet's weave

Millenary
Is a type of
Quest for truth in a dangerous, illusory world,
The beauty & ferocity of setting a hat atop
One's highest point—and the human urge to tame
Rage—trudging endless flights of steps:

Detritus of nightmare.

The castle steams through clanking landscape. The castle's peripatetic,
But that's incidental. What landscape doesn't change/move? Vibrate? Violate?

A filmmaker broadcasts light to evoke memory & impresses the loop on a spindle.
When she's almost asleep the light shuts off and it plays exactly like before, pricks
her. She falls in love. (asleep)

A young girl turns into an elderly lady
What girl doesn't magically grow/age/shrink/darken?

Her mask: a hellish flight of stairs—never-ending ending.
Yo–Yo

Action: She tries to leave the hat shop but each time she opens the door it leads back to itself. Finally she ends up taking refuge at the moving castle. She knows immediately that she's in the traveling castle (moving picture), though she might as well be in the hat shop because the door never opens to where she expects.

She might as well be in his arms. In this poem. Might as well
Be a character in a film—an illusion in an illusion—in my mirror.
Yo–Yo

She is the sister destined to inherit a hat shop, the youngest and therefore most effective in seeking her fortune. Though unable to talk. Have I mentioned that?

Dialogue: (Listen!)

Distant sound of bird vowel
Aural trace of girl shrinking

If she were anyone other than me; for instance, if she were a baker, she'd make bluebird pies and hide in them magic keys and circular saws to free herself from prison (this spell / life). (These words that make her
Myo-kai) (She'd break it like a loaf of bread—steam rising and melting in the surrounding cool.)

 MOONBIRD

Note wing bars, yellow eye,
Like a prairie dog balanced on hind legs
Dreaming of waltzes through cloud-strewn forests,
Rain forests, as-far-as-the-eye-can-rest forests.
Wind re-sizes him. During cyclones
He's rapt in the swallow cycle, gulped down by a cow,
Catfish, chia pet, or hunts blue-jellied beetles
Sweet!
He might be spotted by a local elf,
Owlet, or a luminescent moth that flies in the shadow of his diaphanous wing.
During spectral migration he fades outright
Rarely enters our region
Except during moonlit drive-ins
When nearing an integral scene.

Oshimai [The End]

One April morning, the mother believes she awakens and her lovely daughter has disappeared. The mother has been watching a movie about a young girl, her daughter, with aubergine hair and round eyes. Parasitic bugs that have found solace in the skin of the girl replace her. Upon seeing the parasites, the mother falls into a deep weeping, keening slumber, and the bugs continue her dream. She can exist only through the parasites' memory. They watch her sleep. She supposes she's dead, dreaming that her daughter is directing insects in an anime movie. She's at the movies with secretions that dissemble when light's switched on (the secretions which are raised from light, the secretions which are her thoughts). The viewer will open his eyes and go home (open his heart)—turn on the light—(close his eyes)—dream—(turn in sleep)—become something other—a moth maybe, nothing more substantial than the filmic flame, gossamer, a damselfly's shimmering whirr. Strangers in our body. Passengers. Parasites.

New Poems

Quotations

> *"I am inclined to believe there is no such thing as repetition. And really how can there be."*
> —Gertrude Stein, "Portraits and Repetitions"

> *"Every book is a quotation; and every house is a quotation out of all forests and mines and stone-quarries; and every man is a quotation from all his ancestors."*
> —Ralph Waldo Emerson,
>   *Representative Man*, "Plato; or, the Philosopher"

She particularly enjoyed the edges of woods,
The ledges and shelves, cracks / the fall of the voice /
The crevice in which it lingers
And languishes

The rise and fall of empires, the cycles of cosmology

…particularly enjoyed the edges of words,
Their serrated blades, their gaps / how she fell down in them
When she spoke too fast / the fall of the voice / crevices of silence

The last berry on a branch

…particularly enjoyed the distance between difference and sameness,
An illusion of space, like a mirror reflecting no object, no subject,
How by perceiving gaps, a profound closeness was realized
Of who they were in their listening and their speaking

"History does not repeat itself, but it does rhyme"

The rhyme of personality; its insistence on expression

The rhyme of rhythm

...particularly enjoyed the insistence of lulling water, bird calls or peepers,
Intimate tones. The sounds she envelops, that envelop her. A gong, a vibrating
Cat, sound of a noun, a lullaby liaising with wind, wash in the light rain,
The motor in her intestines, the way sound grounds her,
Grinds out of her, identifies her fallibility, a bottle of fluids. Bottles
On a shelf. Puppets. Marionettes. There is no repetition, Gertrude Stein said.
Only in the stagnant can it exist, and what is stagnant? Even the dead rot

When looking at sound, what do you see? When looking around.

Sound sleep. Sound mind.
Sun warming the morning.
Words stored in a safe.
It is night again, and she walks through the woods,
His home. Words pine and stand.
And then morning, and then night. There is no repetition.

How many times does one tell the same tale? A thousand and one nights...
A hundred and eight echoes...

She speaks two languages—one to communicate, the other
An Esperanto of the heart, the language that doesn't miss a beat.
In the other, words are not always words as one is wont to identify woods.
In other words, sometimes they're misshapen animals,
Sometimes they're hoots. Pictographs. An abrupt thumping of
Roiled space, shivering. Language
Of body—frenetic and dancing.
Its silent pictures. Sentient tinctures. Voiceless shrills. Trills.
Though fight-or-flight triggers the sympathetic nervous system
And praying or counting breath
Binds us to birds, to sound.

In one story, he had echolalia, echopraxia
In one, he had face blindness (prosopagnosia)
Because it is the *face* that triggers memory
The sound of one's face
The space that identifies one's language speed,
Language always running from the door of the mouth,
Returning…

The robin dancing on worms, dancing on the dead

Anyone can resemble anyone

Anyone can have echopraxia, echolalia

It is impossible to speak and listen without embracing one's oneness with others and one's otherness with one

It is impossible to live without embracing one's oneness with others and one's otherness with one

It's impossible to kill without embracing one's oneness with others and one's oneness with one

Transitioning at such speed that one cannot say when one is one or another,
When one is Emerson or Plato,

If the ocean is traveling to or away from the shore

Where transitional surfaces evolve, become more one than the other

The longest wave vanishing, resurfacing on one's face,

In one's song, in one's Stein, in one's bird, one's firstborn,
One bound on a journey away and toward one

Birth and death…bird and dino

Spells of the wind spilling whispers into a well

Will-o'-the-wisp alighting on a liquid horizon

Mutilated mother, muted mother.

Our mother tongue.

Pond Animals

We live in a cage of light
An amazing cage
Animals Animals without end
        —Ikkyū

He brushes the Heart Sutra onto seashells and tosses them into the pond. "Form is no other than emptiness, emptiness no other than form."
      The waving, wielding, yielding,
   booming fluid that is puddle, companion of moon, compassion of moon;
      heartbreaking atmosphere swallows the seashells in the
     perfect wisdom of the moment, of the moon, in the ancient pond
     beyond,
    To the other shore…
Though it is frozen, melting, dripping, Animals Animals dripping from within…Pond without end…

   Something is swimming across her, and then there's the swooping, the shimmying

In every Japanese garden, there is a pond. Weeping willows and black pines.
   Water's edge. Darting turtles, daring

In every human being, there is a pond. Weeping and pining. Her edge. Her ledge.

                                    Her daring.

                         *

Jorge Luis Borges recognized that his inner animal had nearly expired. While in his younger years, he was a monkey, now he had turned into a tired old moose. The first sign of the metamorphosis was his losing his black, then the reds; his last color was yellow. And one day, our hero awoke to realize he had become his mother's dream.
                                                          It was her eyes that kept him.

Wittgenstein's *Remarks on Colour* was written while he was dying of stomach cancer. Stalked by death, he was a sheep cat. Little sleep cat. The lame one. The lamb.

    Fading colors, farming colors

    Kafka asked for his work to be exsanguinated upon his death. Defenestrated. The waning breath of his words not to be bled out, tossed, singed, torched, not humiliated by bylaws and red tape

    Once the growl is gone. A soft resting place. Elephant intelligence. The grief.

*

She spots the cup of pond on the night table. The table has slipped into a dream, and she buries her nose into the lovely pond and, with her paw, sends ripples deep into her animal. A guttural noise in the forest, yonder, that's buried in the body on the bed, in the bed of her body. The ground rolls over, and, as she leaps to safely, the pond follows her onto the floor,

So the dead can ride over rivers…into the sun,
Wearing their horse bone suits

Her death closet filled with ancient helmeted heads,
                                                             Water monsters

A body of standing water, a standing body. Water gardens are ponds as are solar gardens of thermal water. Vernal ponds spend some of the dry season not as ponds. Though even when waterless, they might be referred to as a basket of fluid,
    they might be referred to as ponds.
The ones that are most deeply hidden are touched by sunlight or a person
    Walking through them without being submerged. Ponds as ponds and ponds
        Not as ponds but as puddles reached into and turned into ponds
        By light and life
        Ponds turned inside out

Once ponds sculpted the moon, the moon of his eyes filled
With jellified orbs—He saw
Amebas and seahorses and starfish and multiverses
Singing above and beyond this shore…Animals Animals without end…

Monstrosity: The Goddess Suite

The goddess of Modess
                      Creatrix of Dominatrix

No trace of mind
In the divine undine,

Most feminine of oceans...

          *

Calculate the speed of waves in a puddle,
The mass of light,
Her reflective energy or darting fish thoughts.

The coral bones her algae emboldens
Green flashes / blue flashes—Seaweed negligee
And shipwreck memory.

Lace her tail in the Milky Way.
Her serpent head peering above perfect deep
Foamy crests—the ocean's vagina dentata.

Open your mouth to taste.
Our teeth: vestigal Thalassa!
                      Iron bride

Spacious alchemical vessel for trancing
                  Pelican and serpent
                          Ö

      The great wheel or antithetical moon,
            Antibiotical moon, symbolic colloquial moon—
      Rules for finding the true moon, for recognizing the false moon.

  *

There's the giant devilina who murders hirsute mermaids
The one who steals lobster and love from loathsome fishermen
The spirit who licks untidy bathtubs
The rain-making female nymph
The rain-taking MILF
The shape-shifting hag who lurks in the dunes
In the dark, near the teakettle sorceress
And the demoness of octopi—
Fathoming ocean spills with magick trickery
                Amorphous (Morpheus's surge)
And the mechanical gravity pump (the heart)—

    Mountain of paradise, fountain inferno.

(Her aqueous descendants out the window: Fukushima butterflies /
Beating the air with their grass-blue wings)

The mutated butterfly as the initial condition that caused the tsunami

The tsunami that devastated the forest in her dream

A million stars crazed by a hair's breath

*

Like munching on sun's shadow,
                        The tail end of infinity

          Look! A ship in a light bulb
          Sinking at sea, shinning
          Under the peony moon.

Mappa Mundi of the Uncharted Sea

(Song to My Ancestors)
To penetrate our hydrosphere,
The fathomer must plumb memory
Moment by moment, mile after mile, must calculate the depth
Of a line of sound
Submerged in a pitcher of ocean,
Pouring wave after gravity wave into a tide-pool glass and starfish sky.

Shallow fractal shells on ocean shelves
Lace down the tapered back of black abyss,
And classical strains wend violinistic Okeanós
—The fathomer's unconscious and unmapped ardor or water.
In the quiet of the sea, bioluminescence drifting
              Past the deep knees of liquidity.

Our ancestors' passive lower lair, where time and density clash with destiny

Our ancestors of alchemy energy, following the marine mammals' lineage of light.

At first, underwater habitats and habits were hard to habituate
Plummeting

Subsurface ribbons and angels and eels, elephant seals.
The fathomer must have felt her ancient fish, scaly flesh

The continuous body of earth's blood. (oceanic heat bath)

To make it work, they had to stop thinking
Of themselves as individuals
Who ever lived
On land.

To make it worse,

Prostrate before Ondine with whiskey and wine

They had to stop thinking as individuals.

(*Memory of an Oceanic Party Girl*)
Earthlings lost the shell game, a confidence trick that overconfidence
Tricked them into buying into
When air expired.

At goddess correspondence school, I traded in my fur for Neoprene

Despite what had been trending, there wasn't a planet B,
So the earthlings dove into the sea,
Made their home in earth unknown,
Lemurring into under-life without demurring.

Jump!

There is no sound here. No light. No autumn leaves.
Ocean without sausage, no derma
For the golem,
                Only that great encompassing stream, compassionate
Scream or omphalos—

The fathomers scale
The longest mountain chain in this vast, tireless multiverse

Multiloss vest of life

Strung around the neck of the sea,
Buoyancy of diamonds, carbuncles, our most precious colonies.

The Woods

The blue woods, the milkweed meadow woods, woods thick, woods night. Reams of dreaming woods. Vast woods in a dram of spirits. Mangrove woods with crabs and spiders. Mangroves with gators. Webs wending spirals between viny shelves for shells and schools of skeleton fish, anchored in mud, anchored in mind. Virgins and terrapins. Tarantulas and slugs. What in the world is not in the woods?

Everyone you love is in the woods.

Mother tells you Auntie's heart is bad, that it has run amok. You hear this as *a band of bandits heisted Auntie's heart, removed it from her chest and locked it in a chest in the woods.* You hear this as *Auntie's woods is in her heart.*

When you hear with your eye, for the first time, the woods will become intimate.

There are woods you walk through every day.

Sometimes you are aware of the woods and some days you don't notice.

Mother tells you Auntie's hungry, she's scared of the dark, she's scared of death, scared to death. Mother gives you a wicker basket and scoots you out the mahogany door, the door that leads straight to the woods.

As you walk the woods, the fetid fragrance smells like Auntie's putrefying flesh. The eyes of the woods are yellow irises. The teeth of the woods are like arrowheads.

You go in search of your auntie's heart. Her dark, sick heart. In the heart of the woods.

You go in search of Auntie's dreams.

One goes for one thing and returns with something else.

One learns in the dark. One sees and hears differently there. One fills one's pockets with the dark.

You do not want to close your eyes. It's dark in the woods. You ask Mother to keep the stars on, you ask for the moon to be your nightlight. You ask to take a dog with amber eyes that shine like the Lupus constellation, a seeing-eye dog that seizes small prey in the dark. You pray in the woods. It is your altar. You burn sweet sage, and you change in the woods. The woods is your alter ego.

You dress as a glowing worm in the woods. You become an oak, a mighty oak with red squirrels swirling down your limbs and branches. Your roots tangle in the earth of the woods. You learn the language of frogs in the woods. In the dark, scary woods you find your powers, your potions, your prowess. You learn the language of woods and find that it is not foreign. There are no foreign words in the woods.

When you enter the woods, when you breathe woods' air as you exhale the woods, as you become the woods, your heart is no longer your heart.

When you enter the woods, you are alone; your heart races through your inner woods.

When you enter the woods, you aim to walk through the woods, you aim to find Auntie and then you aim to return to a place that is anti-woods, that is non-woods, you aim to return home. You believe your home is not the woods. You believe your home is Auntie.

When you enter the woods your bones begin to ache. The boles sway. Trees nurse. When you enter the woods, your breath turns wet and life thrives from the air you share with the woods, the air you offer the woods.

When you enter the woods, you become the woods, you become its food. The heart that oxidizes your blood becomes the woods' thousand and eight hearts. The sweat pouring from your brow becomes its dew. Your amber irises become the woods' flowers. You are the woods' blood as you race through the woods.

Of course you get lost in the woods, of course you can't leave the woods—that is the nature of woods. Auntie got lost in the woods, wrote of the woods, sang woods words, woods worlds. Whorls of woods. Woods moons, woods dogs. Woods creep into buildings, spies of woods fly in the sky, expanding woods by night, disguising woods by day. Even if you extinguish all the wind of the woods, all the rings of the woods, there'd be books made of woods, libraries of trees, all singing woods' paeans, inks of woods and atlases, clothes pins and plastics, film and fabric, all rhizomes connecting to the woods—all roads, all roots, leading there.

A Thousand and One Gretels: Alone in the Wood

A small gang of Gretels runs off,
        Are run out of town,
  Find an emerald world,
        The Wild West of witches,
             A candy city,
    A wealth beyond the Gretel Gang's wildest wishes.

Once upon a time there were naughty, naughty gamines—A gang of girls!
                 A gaggle of Gretels!
And when they shot through Munchkin, Kansas, you bet your sweet butt,
Dot hiked up her gingham
       And tore off behind them on a pink Harley.

Sometimes, though, the cyclone doors of her mind would fly open,
And stepmothers stepped out into her hourglass,
         ...Looking glass,
              The glass slipper,
And flying monkeys would corner the sagging, aging girl in the gang,
     Would corner the girl alone.

How to get free from all that wind?
        —For instance, falling down a rabbit hole,
  Holing up in a fallout shelter,

     Losing her way,
        Her mind.

How to get free of the storybook,
                               From believing
At the center of the storm,
                Mama's pulling strings,
                            Father's making a living,
She: snug in her just-right-sized bed, convalescing
       —*It's like a switch clickin' off in my head,* Dot says, a dot
                  Of dust in the tornado that's blowing through
    Where mind is
              Realized, anxiety of the body drops away
    With delusion (no wood, no witch, no which way would the yellow brick
               road wind)
And all of a sudden there's peace.

The clickin' of poppies.
Clickin' her heels together.
Clickin' her way home.

Fringe

Let's say time is a moving container, like a train
Holding various replicants simultaneously,
Like a TV set on wheels carrying *Fringe* and *X-Files*;
Let's say characters and plot lines quantum leap into the viewer's gray matter

Questions are raised about how one exists in the same space on separate frequencies

Multiple tracks of cellular structures
Variable planes
Traveling at a shared speed

If there's an Observer
A server
A surveillance camera
An eye toward clarity

Questions are raised about aliens among us, within us.

Having missed her appointment show
To remotely wander the medieval TV cathedral,
She returns to regularly scheduled programming,
Though how long might she be absent before what she views
Does not resemble what she expects?
Before similarities
Are synchronicities
Without a memory chip of their previous similitude?
Before bridges between streams collide?

In order to wipe the world from mind immemorial—

After it was cancelled
Midplot, exiled to reruns
Or Nietzschean eternal recurrence, she turned on
A word building class held in the world building—
A conworld of deception
In TiVo time

After all, the brain seems to adjust to the annihilation of species
And cancelled series,
Characters evanescing from airwaves
Or transforming inside window frames that look onto alternative situations,
Our fragmented inner-light projections

Like looking in a darkened mirror, a flattened space with submerged depth—

There, questions arise about authenticity, about which realm is reality,
About what reality to watch.

Suicide by Cartoon

She collects broken critters,
                    Ones who plunge off cliffs,
            Varmints with dagger-pierced
                    Livers, others critters who hurl through
      Windshields at the edge of playgrounds,
                    Critters who pick themselves up, dust themselves off,
Turn to dust and back to radiant light.

Ashes to ashes
Reel to reel

It's a falcon under the bridge.
            With no children in the fairytale,
                          The forest is confused.
    Bands of dead moms
                Wander the wooded heart of fetid grave groves.
It rains all the time. Too many toadstools.
      Peach pits spit on a growling ground.
      No do-overs, they're gone gone.

Dust to dust

She was beside herself,
            both selves were
                        Peering and disappearing,
A black-and-white cow skitters across
                A moon-eye aperture,
          Recoiling into the lightless barrel of night.
                Boom!!!

In the midst of life we are in death

John's Koan

I was told Welsh rarebit gives one obstreperous dreams
And before I knew it, I was clad in a balaclava and on a grid
Of unplotted nights. I would have brought you along
If I could, though I suspected anything might have happened
On the say-so of Frank O'Hara, who was on the down-low. The upshot being
The meadow was closed for business, and the Committee
Raised the motion that we live our lives
Minus our assignations. The chair, of course, emphasizing
The precise reason for this experiment
Might come at any time, like a cloudless sky, open
To interpretation or weather. As it happened, Mom was so piping hot
She stabbed me in the armpit. That transpired six thousand miles
From this world. Six minutes ago. I had suspected
The firehouse was a cathedral or a launching pad of sorts. Stained glass and sirens,
Never mind the clerestory. Never mind the secret machinations,
Which revolved around ingénues, shuttlecocks, and lost causes.
Before I knew it, the dream subsided,
Kind of like a passing flu or light hitting an ocean
Wave. Yeah, there's a shore, a story, a storm, and the dhow and shoal
Are breezeways to carry you here; a little leap
Will do the trick. If not for Cousin It, you would never
Be in my life. An auspicious sleight of hand, don't you think?

The Day Lou Died

Innumerable people wrote this poem
on October 27, 2013...because of Frank O'Hara's
"The Day Lady Died," written on July 17, 1959
for Billie. And Lou wrote "Lady Day," and I was born in January '59,
and, in his poem, Frank was taking the Long Island Railroad to Easthampton.
It took him a little longer to get there—from the city—
than it would have on the day Lou died. I started *this* poem
on November 19, not October 27, the day Lou died.
I'm not proud it took me three weeks to start a poem that countless others
managed to write on the right day. Nick Flynn's was published in the *New Yorker*
before I typed (processed) my first word. Maybe this poem should be
called "The Day Reed Didn't Die" because he didn't die today, and I wasn't able
to write on the day he did, even though I thought
about it and knew everyone else was working on theirs.
I was too lazy, too sad, too involved
in watching Lou YouTubes and surfing Facebook,
e-checking what my "Friends" were posting about Lou.
It was a mass cyber-mourning. Frank died at forty,
Billie at forty-four. Lou died
in Springs, which is part of Easthampton.
I spend summers in Montauk. Frank, me, and Candy traveling the LIE,
singing Lou songs...not really, just in this poem. In *his* poem,
Frank wrote, "beginning to sun," while Lou wrote, "...beginning to see
the light."
      Today is November 29
the day after Thanksgiving, and I'm still working
on these damn lines, thinking of him, of how the poem lingers on,
and his songs...all alone and lonely.

Bird Calls

      Birth calls, growling tigers of the mind

Who isn't formed of scraps of all types?

Emily Dickinson died at fifty-five. Thich Nhat Hanh says because we believe we come from nothing and vanish into nothing,
                          we live with the fear of annihilation,
of no beginning and no end.
            So many years ago, at the (h)Ear Inn, Jackson Mac Low's resonance loosed in the atmosphere.
          His reverberations in my poems, mine in his, his blanketing NYC. Once a student took me aside and claimed another student was stealing her words.

"Who understands any of this?" Jackson once said at The Project. "Who understands?" I hear it now. The question that hovers over all language. Such a racket made by those who have passed, who haven't stopped screaming.

The little gate flies open

You put your brown circles in a basket; they are curls

I carry along with my needles and yarn and pens.

I miss the grasshopper

The gilliflowers
            Sleep in the hair of the hills

The air dressed in white gowns. It is January, 1859. Martine

Will be born in one hundred years. She is asleep through this realm

Though is elsewhere—the hinges: of doors, between states and friends,

Cabinets of dreams, perennials, and architects' pencils.

I directed her to the cemetery to save her time and expense

Laconic loons   oceanic noons

When Martine Bellen is born

Dear Ones

She will have forgotten the kind and hallowed feeling of dying,
The fiction of pain and poetry,
Dickinson's unloaded gun and pinafores

Eight moons dressed the ruby-black velvet night. Let's talk about death and what it has to do with poetry. Some Martines might argue that they are unrelated (though what is unrelated?), that poetry proves more robust than death, doesn't abide by its laws, resides outside of death's realm, is blind to death's fifty faces, that poetry alters with styles while death does not, that poetry is older than death itself, that death is more forgiving, inclusive than poetry, that poets don't die, that death doesn't sing

Sinew
Syntax
Synapse
Apse of a church
Asp of the earth
Its membrane of the heart

Death poems, knells,

The spontaneity of koans

The formlessness of moans

The stinking breath of both

Everything can be a trap. Even the poem, even the koan, even death, even its opposite. Everything can be a treasury. It can't be language if it's translatable. If you transfer all the words of the poem (all the waves of an ocean) to other sounds (an alternate body of water) and the poem remains…
Mind as the ocean, its waves, its ways

Grains of fine sand…prose or poetry?

Identifying oneself as a poet might be like identifying oneself as a cat trainer or exotic dancer, not a door-to-door vacuum salesman. For instance, if you meet a handsome stranger at a bar and he asks you who you are, and you answer a cat trainer who dances exotically, he / she (the prosy one) will think you are toying with him. He will turn paler than light lilacs. His uncertainty will verge on poetry—he might no longer be one or the other. Like discarding roosters at night to avoid calamity. Like shaking your fist as though it's a plump peony on a weak stem. You might send him a scrapbook, a letter that's a credo in disguise. You might hand him a flower, and he'll break trying to maintain it. He will avoid you the next time he sees you through the mirror over the bar; he will pretend you are not there; he will not believe you are *you*; he will be convinced you are a writer of fiction, a rewriter of form, a reformer. He will not realize he is a subject of a poem, that the poem mixes forms—human, plastic, organic, nonsentient—like the martini he drinks in a lady-shaped glass. It can't be helped because of Shakespeare and his witches, because of Dickinson and her body of floating epistolary. Form is a hybrid in every situation/moment. He will look at himself through the mirror that frames the bar, and he will wonder if he is a translation of a poem that got mixed in with prose…

A mixologist of spirits. Though why isn't one enough for some—look to Murasaki Shikibu, look to Emily Dickinson—look to space-time, to Master Dogen's Being-Time and ku-ku (space), look to John Cage…

Why is form empty, impermanent—why can't poetry stay poetry and fiction stay prose!

If one thinks of space-time as prose, what then is poetry? Timeless-spaceless. And mixed together? What happens to stymied space-time when poetry and prose mate?

On the hinge of life and death, though as alive as when he took his first breath, he recites his death novel:
Takuan wrote 夢 before leaving. *Dream.* Only 夢.

Though some are traitors.
Velvalee Dickinson spied for Japan during World War II, using dolls to transport her messages. In encrypted letters, ostensibly about dolls, she'd send classified information—One of these three dolls was an old fisherman with a net over his back, another an old woman of wood

In *Spring and All*, W.C.W. writes: "The form of prose is the accuracy of its subject matter—how best to expose the multiform phases of the material…

The form of poetry is related to the movements of the imagination revealed in words—or whatever it may be—"

In a letter, Emily wrote: A mutual plum is not a plum. W.C.W.: so sweet and so cold

A confession to his wife of his thievery

Some writers are traitors and thieves. Audre Lorde said to me, "All poets are liars."

———

Emily's letters turned to poetry when she abandoned the quotidian, the situation (space-time), when the butterfly hinge swings

She said, "Robins are my dolls"

Space skin or skin and space or skin space (skin milk)—the porous line where we permeate, how we become traitors (Barbara says some of her poet friends eye her suspiciously for writing fiction). The question might be asked: When is language only poetry or only prose? When is form one or the other? The absolute and the relative. How to tame a bird.

"Like two arrow points that touch high in the sky"

Two days before the 108 gongs (the new year will begin—the old one ends, vanishes into nothingness…how can this be so?), rings of sound beginning their yearly migration, their helix of flight, their murmuration…

MARTINE BELLEN (martinebellen.com). Martine Bellen is the author of nine collections of poetry including *GHOSTS!* (Spuyten Duyvil); *The Vulnerability of Order* (Copper Canyon Press); *Tales of Murasaki and Other Poems* (Sun & Moon), which won the National Poetry Series Award; and the novella *2X²* (BlazeVOX [BOOKS]). Her bilingual collection, *Musée Magie*, has been published in Germany by Verlag Waldgut (translator, Hans Jürgen Balmes). She has written the libretto for *Ovidiana*, an opera based on Ovid's *Metamorphoses* (composer, Matthew Greenbaum), which was performed in New York City and Philadelphia. She collaborated with David Rosenboom on *Ah! Opera No-Opera*, a collective work, co-composed and performed by creators from around the globe. Its world premiere was at REDCAT in L.A (for more information, visit www.ah-opera.org). She has co-written, with Zhang Er, the libretto of *Moon in the Mirror: A Monodrama*—composer, Stephen Dembski—based on the Chinese legend of Chang E. She has been a recipient of the Queens Art Fund, New York Foundation for the Arts, the Fund for Poetry, and the American Academy of Poets Award, and has received a residency from the Rockefeller Foundation at the Bellagio Center. Bellen is a contributing editor of the literary journal *Conjunctions*.

www.ingramcontent.com/pod-product-compliance
Lightning Source LLC
Chambersburg PA
CBHW081333080526
44588CB00017B/2613